Within A Purple Heart ...

*... through the Battle of the Hüertgen Forest
and Prison Camps of the Second World War*

The Personal Story of Daniel A. Farchione, Sr.

Written by Sharon Farchione-Ross

Published by Shining Purple Publishing.

Printed and bound in the United States of America

ISBN: 978-0-615-23498-4

Library of Congress Catalog Card Number pending

First Printing — December 2008
Second Printing — June 2009

Book design by Greene Design Group

Order additional copies from:
     Sharon Farchione-Ross
     Rochester, New York
     (585) 802-8440
     sfarchio@rochester.rr.com

*A portion of the proceeds from this book will be donated
to the Military Order of the Purple Heart,
the Military Ex-Prisoners of War Foundation, Inc.
and other veteran organizations.*

Daniel and Sharon
dedicate this book
to
Mimi Farchione

To my loving, beautiful wife, best friend and lifelong partner …
I am ever so grateful for Mimi's love, faith and devotion.
She stood by my side through it all. Even when we
were not able to be physically together, we were joined in heart
and spirit. She has suffered with me, cried with me,
laughed with me and rejoiced with me.
Mimi, words cannot describe what you truly mean to me and
the depths of my gratitude. I am proud to say that this story is
not just mine — it is ours. My life with you is an endless love
song. Our spirits are eternally connected in harmony. I love you.
— Daniel

To my loving, wise, courageous mother …
a woman of grace and dignity.
My mother has given so much of herself to her family.
Through her love, faith, hard work and diligent prayers
including many rosaries, she has been nourishing,
inspiring and uplifting us throughout the years.
Mom, I love you. I am so thankful for your fervent
love that was a beacon of light strengthening Dad
and guiding him home. Your wisdom and guidance
on being a woman, wife and mother is a life treasure.
Thank you for teaching me how to love by living your love
for Dad and our family through your actions.
— Sharon

In loving memory of Salvatore and Sara Farchione whose
bright spirits moved through the writing of this book. In
gratitude for the family legacy of courage, perseverance, dignity,
selflessness, faith and unconditional love that they illuminate.

Table of Contents

Acknowledgements

To think of a section devoted to "thank you" initially brought some concern around my abilities to find the words to encapsulate the meaning and significance of those involved in this project. I believe that faith and gratitude are the essence of healing and living our wholeness. To enjoy our freedom we must properly recognize and appreciate those who sacrificed and gave so much to make it happen. A work such as this is not complete without the recognition of all those who were a part of this book. The journey of writing brings an array of peaks and valleys. The words and actions of support and encouragement from those whose enthusiasm fed the momentum, have been integral in the completion of this book. These expressions of faith and gratitude, that have been extended in many forms and fashions, illustrate and perpetuate healing and wholeness for all of us. With heartfelt gratitude, I would like to acknowledge:

Virginia Greene Conn, who demonstrated extraordinary gentle patience and guidance. Thank you, Virginia, for the tender loving care and expertise you infused in the organization, design and creation of this book. Our harmonious communication and your stamina, especially while fine tuning the manuscript, has truly been a blessing.

Ramsey Raybeck, for her earnest editing. Thank you Ramsey for all of your efforts in "cleaning it up" within some tight time constraints.

Steve Cole, for creating a beautiful cover with Virginia. Thank you Steve for sharing your gifts, especially for illustrating my father's vision for the cover with such artistic clarity.

Rev. Lisette Maginn, for brief but powerful literary consultations. Thank you for taking the time to give me honest and very helpful feedback, support and guidance.

Gerry Gears, my brother-in-law, who painstakingly worked long hours to meet a timeline. Thank you Gerry for the beautiful work in miraculously restoring the photos to a printable quality and for your efforts in organizing and saving family photos.

My sisters and brother, **Mary Jean Gears, Joanne Davis, Linda Farchione-Janczak, Donna Williams and Daniel Farchione, Jr.** for their support and input along the way. Thank you all for your prompt responses to my inquiries and in sharing your reflections and impressions. I greatly appreciate the encouragement.

Joanne Davis, for the many long phone calls. Thank you Joanne for the helpful feedback and the time spent listening, inspiring and encouraging me.

Donna Williams, for promptly responding to the many emails. Thank you, Donna, for your loyal assistance in bringing clarity in moments of confusion.

Sue Ann Walker, for keeping the Farchione Family album. Thank you Sue Ann for responding so quickly and kindly to the call for family photos and for the effort you put into preserving and pictorially recording the extended family legacy.

Gwen Mazza, for her ongoing encouragement and gentle reminders of what she learned from studying with me. Thank you Gwen, for your faith and appreciation and for recognizing my father and mother through your television program.

To numerous family members, friends and colleagues who crossed my path offering words of support. Thank you for your interest and encouragement at critical times. Being too numerous to mention by name, I wish for you all to know how grateful I am for your enthusiasm and kindness.

To all of those who fought in the Battle of the Hüertgen Forest and all military men and women that have fought to uphold our freedom, and their families. Thank you for your courage, patriotism and sacrifices.

To my husband, Michael, and our children, Nessa and Rachel, for their love, faith, support and extra help in keeping it all going. Thank you for the loving patience, wisdom and understanding through the years.

And of course, **Dad and Mom**, for graciously sharing it all and for the time spent, phone calls, emails, manuscript reviews and lunches. Thank you for your courage, editing, honesty, wisdom and selfless giving of yourselves that we may know more about bravery, freedom and love and what makes up who we are today.

Thank you God for answering all prayers and for blessing me with such incredible family, friends and colleagues.

Preface
A Daughter's Reflections

On Thanksgiving Day, November 23, 2005, my family gathered at the home of my sister and brother-in-law, Joanne and Rick. Amongst the smiling faces and sparkling eyes, we enjoyed the comfort of home and family. Still, sadness hovered, as we were all aware of the absence of my nephew Mathew, a lieutenant in the US Navy. He was serving as a flight officer in Operation Iraqi Freedom.

Revealing a mother's relief, my sister Linda shared that she spoke to Mathew by phone earlier in the day. We noted how remarkable it was, under the circumstances, that she could have any communication with him. Grateful that Mathew was well, we remembered past wars when families were completely cut off from any contact or knowledge of their loved ones in battle. As the rest of the family arrived, the void of Matthew's absence grew more pronounced.

Dinner proceeded with the usual small talk — comments about being full before we started eating, the usual laughter about the competition over whose stuffing is better — and our toast for giving thanks. It was after our salute to Mathew, that my father spoke.

The room was silent. Dad remembered the Thanksgiving that he ate turkey rations in the forest. He told us how appreciative and surprised he was when he found the turkey rations in the supplies. "The forest?!" we asked. "What forest?!" "The Hüertgen Forest," he announced. "The Battle of the Hüertgen Forest — the battle that I am getting the Bronze Star for." With quizzical, widening eyes, the family erupted in harmonic exclamation, "The Bronze Star?!"

The desire to hear Dad disclose the hidden secrets of his war experiences had created a lifetime of unspoken questions. We all needed a moment to grasp the words that were being carried by Dad's voice to our ears.

Then, the questions flooded the table. We wanted to know more. We wanted the missing pieces, the secrets, the elephant in the room that had been such a part of our life, to reveal itself. We knew Dad had a Purple Heart. He recently found out that he was to receive a Bronze Star for the Battle of the Hüertgen Forest. As we asked more questions, he did not dismiss us. He did not avoid the questions. He shared, and we listened intently. The grandchildren had pensive expressions with far away looks as they listened quietly to Grandpa's stories. All seemed to embrace every word in astonishment of how he survived such horrific experiences.

As I heard the words, I sought to grasp the fact that he was actually telling "it." Just this past summer, I had received clarity while praying for my father and nephew. I was asking for improvement in my father's health, as he was suffering from dizziness and excruciating back pain; and for Mathew, who was about to be deployed to Iraq. While in prayer, I experienced what I refer to as Divine Insight, moving my heart to understand the connection between my father's physical symptoms and my nephew going off to war.

Mathew was the first grandson going into battle since Dad fought in World War II, and I noticed how this was triggering Dad's unexpressed feelings about his own war experience. He was harboring these intensifying memories. It was critical for Dad to share his story; to bring him the much needed relief. Moreover, others would benefit from his invaluable wisdom and inspiration.

Compelled to pass this insight on to my father, I immediately reached for my laptop. Before I picked up the phone to call him, the fear of his reaction came flooding in. I imagined that he would reject the information altogether given that the subject had been off limits for so long. Rather than making a cold call to my father, I dialed my sister, Joanne, looking to her for the "go ahead" to call Dad; the voice mail answered.

At that moment I knew, that this was my test. Finally mustering the courage, I called him. To my delightful surprise, he carefully listened as I explained what had happened and read him the information that came to me. He did not resist or blow me off as ridiculous. He even asked me to fax him a copy implying that it was something that needed his attention.

As the days went by, I would periodically remind him of the importance of sharing his story. He agreed and then something would always distract us. It seemed like the motivation was growing weaker.

Only now, do I realize that Dad was wisely waiting for the perfect time to open up. Looking at Mom, sitting so lovingly beside Dad at the Thanksgiving table, I wondered what the war times were like for her. The thought of being apart from her husband, who was serving in the army, while hearing about the deaths of so many soldiers, was incomprehensible to me. How did she cope with the intensity of the emotion? There was so much more that I longed to know; so I asked.

After the holiday, I called Dad to thank him for talking to us about the battle. I asked him about using some of his experiences in another book I was working on. He shocked me once again when he asked me to write a book specifically about his war story. I was thrilled and humbled by his new-found openness.

As time passed, Dad understandably started having second thoughts about reliving his experiences. He also doubted that anyone really wanted to hear it, minimizing the value of his experiences. He felt that others went through so much more than he did.

To assure him of the benefits in writing about his

experiences, I pointed out that he could teach others through example. Neither of my parents seemed to realize that their love, courage, patience, perseverance, appreciation for life and most of all their selflessness was truly impressive.

Sometimes in relationships, there is conflict because of perceived inequality of activities or devotion. Conversely, my parents insist on taking care of each other or doing more for the other. It is clear that their habitual actions of love are all they know — simply a way of life. I am convinced that other families would benefit if more people could know my parents' experiences and how they live love.

This recording has evolved as I was blessed and honored to have many conversations with my father, Daniel Anthony Farchione, Sr. and my mother, Amelia Palumbo Farchione. They are my teachers of love and of life ... they are my heroes.

Daniel, son of Italian-born Salvatore and Sarafina (Sara) Farchione, is a man of great courage and faith, wisdom, compassion and humility. He is a devoted, loving, dancing husband. He is an understanding, fun-loving and brilliant father, grandfather and great-grandfather. He is a visionary, inventor and innovator.

Amelia (Mimi), daughter of Italian-born, Pieter and Antoinette Palumbo, is a wise woman of faith and great strength. She is a devoted wife. She is a loving, playful, giving mother, grandmother and great-grandmother. She is an inspiration and a motivator. She is a visionary.

This is both a war story and a love story of Pfc. Farchione and his wife, Mimi. It is about Daniel's "Purple Heart" beating through the deadly Hüertgen Forest Campaign and strengthening him to triumph over his German prison-camp experience. Daniel's story describes a heart filled with a tremendous faith and love, knowing that he would continually sustained by God's miraculous intervention and presence. Nested within the "Purple Heart" is Mimi, who with a courageous, faithful heart and powerful spirit, endured her own daily battles and suffered with her husband.

As I reflected on my conversations with Dad, I found myself

moving back in time. He was so courageous in his willingness to speak about the memories he had been battling for years. He had overcome the continual reminders of human destruction while focusing on the needs of his family. There were so many years where Dad and Mom faced the residual impact of the war and did not have vital information to help understand what he was going through. I now realize that what I perceived as Dad keeping his experiences a secret, was actually my father taking care of his family as a true soldier. He was protecting us from the ugly, terrors of that life.

With Dad's words defining the war reverberating through me, I realized how fresh these horrors have always been for him. I thought about my childish ways, whining when bored or felt I was being treated unfairly. He was always so patient.

I remembered the one and only time that he sent me to my room. Grumbling about his request for me to get the ketchup, I questioned why 'I always' had to do things instead of my sister. How did he keep his composure? How did he not scream out in a rage-full reaction to my ungrateful fog, oblivious to what he had suffered for my freedom? How did he embrace us with love when we griped and bickered?

Then I thought of my parents as newlyweds being wrenched away from each other. How did they survive the separation? I know the aching feelings when my husband would leave for a trip, even though I knew where he was going and when he would return. What would it be like to have to say goodbye and not know where he was going? How could one move forward not knowing when or if there would ever be a return home?

As I wrote, my heart was filled with the sensations of those moments for my parents. The words I typed blurred as tears suddenly filled my eyes, streaming down my face, as images and impressions of Dad's experiences came to life within me.

Prayers rose from my core, soothing and filling my heart. My prayers, with a hope, a desire, a radiating wish that by experiencing this phenomenon, which somehow put me in those situations with him, the pain and loneliness that bore witness in my father's memories would somehow be relieved.

Chapter 1
Heeding the Call

Images from the past flashed before Daniel as he stared out the window of the train that was rushing him to his last stop on American soil before boarding the ship to an unknown battlefield. The only direction in his life now was towards war. He was unable to turn back to the sweet comforts of home, and he certainly could not stop time or the train.

It was October 17, 1944, the end of the shortest week of Daniel's life. After completing basic training, he had been given one week's leave before deployment overseas. Daniel was panged with flashes of saying goodbye to his dear wife, Mimi and their newborn daughter, Mary Jean. Mimi was too sick to get out of bed since the difficult delivery in September, and he wanted so much to be there to take care of his family.

Daniel struggled to catch his breath and grasp the fact that this was really happening to him. This was not how it was supposed to be. He never thought, on the day he married Mimi, that this would be how they would spend their second wedding anniversary.

Memories of floating down the aisle arm in arm with his beautiful bride drifted through his heart. It was just two years earlier, when the doors of St. Mary's Church in Canandaigua, New York had swung open as Daniel and Mimi, united by their loving vows, stepped out into the world to begin their life together. Their smiling faces shone through the raining downpour as Joe, dressed in his police uniform, proudly held the umbrella over them. It was glorious. An otherwise dreary, rainy day was transformed by their heavenly love, and with celebration, they entrusted their dreams to each other.

Now, feeling the despair of having just been wrenched away from her, he could never have imagined that this journey would force them to the depths of human agony.

Daniel's heart filled the silence of the train car with reminiscences of when he found out that it was his time to go where so many had gone before him. He recalled his happiness that day. Grateful that the work day was over, he had been looking forward to seeing his lovely wife who was carrying their first child. Entering the coziness of home, he whistled one of his father's favorite tunes, harmonizing with the delicious aroma wafting from the kitchen.

"Lucky, lucky me, I'm a lucky son of a gun
I work eight hours, I sleep eight hours,
I have eight hours of fun
Lucky, lucky me, I'm a lucky son of a gun."

Feelings of delight suddenly turned to despair when he spotted the dreaded draft notice waiting for him on the kitchen table. Although he never spoke to Mimi about it, he often reminded himself that this was inevitable.

As he picked up the notice, the faces of the three high school friends who had already been killed in the war drifted through his mind's eye. The relentless memory of all of them talking about enlisting together repeatedly shocked his inner core. He had decided to wait. Remembering growing up with them in grammar school, he realized that he was now the fourth of the five guys in his eighth grade graduating class from St. Mary's School to leave home for the battlefield.

A silent scream erupted from his soul. He was filled with the discomfort of being torn from his loved ones, of not being there for his family. Powerless.

Daniel felt for his wife, his daughter, his mother and father, and his younger brother. Daniel had always looked out for Patrick, who was hearing impaired, often guiding him in a sometimes cruel "hearing world" that so often misunderstood those who were unable to hear. He had shared so much with Patrick and they had learned from each other.

Feeling so thankful for his family, the thought of not being with them elicited an unbearable emotional volcano. From deep within Daniel a scream erupted— and again — as when he first saw the draft notice. It was a silent scream, a scream that he vowed he would never let his wife hear.

Daniel returned to the solace of his memories. He struggled to push his feelings away as he anticipated doing what many of his fellow countrymen were doing: leaving home to defend the country. Knowing the need to accept this responsibility, he kept telling himself that freedom was of the utmost importance. Preserving it had to be his first priority. He was a man. He was a soldier. He must be brave.

Daniel could not stop wondering what it was going to be like to be on a battlefield. He remembered the stories from a family friend who had fought in the Pacific. The words warning him that he better hope he did not have to go to the Pacific rang in his ears. He recognized the great courage it had taken for his parents to leave the familiarity of their home in Italy to come to America. Now he was being called to play his part in defending the freedom of this land of opportunity enjoyed by his family in their adopted country. It was something he had to do.

Daniel looked down at his arms and legs, hoping they did not reveal his trembling insides. He wondered how he could possibly pull a trigger and hit a human target with fear shaking every fiber of his being. He thought of the discussions in basic training when the soldiers talked about their uneasiness with killing, especially when receiving bayonet and hand-to-hand combat techniques. What will it be like? Worse yet, he thought, what will it be like to be shot at and to actually be face to face, hand-to-hand with the enemy? What would it be like to take a last breath, and die on a cold, lonely battlefield, in a foreign country; thousands of miles away from home...home... home...

Again and again Daniel's thoughts were drawn back to the stinging awareness of how much he did not want to leave his family. He realized that he had never spoken to Mimi aloud about his fears. It was his time to do what so many others had done without complaining. Everyone just did what they had to do. Mimi did what so many loved ones had been doing; helping a husband or son prepare to leave for the service. They all suffered silently.

Indeed, Daniel and Mimi lived united in love. They both knew the intense inner battle that would be encountered each day they were apart. They sensed the terror raging within the other and wanted to spare each other the sight of their tears. The heavy sadness overflowed from their hearts.

Daniel's heart was soothed when they had prayed together. He was confident that in parting they left each other with the best — strength in faith and love.

He reflected on Mimi's stamina and inspiring spirit. While he was in basic training, Mimi set up a hair styling area on the back porch. Daniel smiled as he envisioned how proud she was of her success and how proud he was of her.

She had been pregnant during most of his time in basic training. He felt so badly that he was not able to take care of her during those precious months. He was so thankful to his younger brother, Fred, who was always ready to help. He diligently rode his bike to Mimi's every day after dinner to help her with chores and keep her company. Never complaining about what he was missing out on as a teenager, Fred was always willling to do something for the family.

Daniel pondered his wife's courage and phenomenal strength in the miraculous birth of Mary Jean on September 15, 1944. He was grateful to his sister-in-law, Mary, who had called to check on her when she was five weeks overdue. After hearing that the doctor in Waterloo had ignored Mimi's concerns, she insisted on bringing her to Canandaigua. Mary immediately took her to the doctor who had delivered Mimi 24 years earlier on Christmas

Day. Planning on admitting her to the hospital at 9:00 a.m. the next morning, the physician advised her to stay at Mary's for the night.

After a very difficult labor 12 hour labor, Mary Jean was born. Mimi was not able to leave the delivery room until 10:30 p.m. The doctor, Mary and her mother, Antoinette, stayed with Mimi until 4:30 the next morning. Antoinette, who continued to speak her native language of Italian, sat in the corner of Mimi's room repeating the rosary. At one point when Mimi opened her eyes, she saw a glow coming from the upper corner of the room, where she then saw a vision of the Blessed Mother. Despite her severe physical and emotional discomfort, she was then able to rest.

The next day the doctor reported that had Mimi gone one more day, both she and the baby would have died. The difficult delivery required that the new mom and baby spend two weeks in the hospital. Mimi was confident that they had received Divine protection.

Daniel gratefully contemplated all the miracles his family had been blessed with. His heart savored the moments during the past week when he was able to embrace his wife and hold his baby daughter. Since Mimi was still recovering from childbirth, they all stayed with her sister, Mary. What a joy it was to hold Mary Jean for the first time. He was enraptured by her beautiful face. He wanted nothing more than to marvel at her.

They decided to have Mary Jean baptized during that week. Because of the restricted time, the only day to have the baptism was the Sunday before Daniel was to leave. The baptism began Daniel's week with such a sweet day as the family gathered to celebrate. Daniel's heart ached with wishes that the day did not have to end.

There was so much love and joy as everyone feasted on an abundance of delectable Italian cuisine. Daniel especially appreciated the hugs, smiles and laughter that were woven throughout the delicious food. He savored the nourishment that filled his heart, soul and body, giving him the courage for his journey.

5

Commanded to maintain military silence regarding his destination, all Daniel could say was that he was leaving to serve in the war. No one knew where he was going. Family and friends searched for the words of encouragement, faith and strength, without really talking about "it." Daniel moved through the rounds of goodbyes, silently wishing for a reprieve, but time pushed him forward.

Before he knew it, he was waking up on the day he was scheduled to leave. A day he would never forget. With his heart growing heavier and heavier, he moved through the last few hours before the forced separation from his family. Suddenly, he found himself sitting in the car, driving away from waving hands, floating kisses and tear filled eyes.

Despairingly, Daniel was leaving behind all that he knew and loved with no idea of what he was about to face. His mind held on so tightly to the last hug, the last kiss, the last sight of Mimi, Mary Jean, his parents, sisters, brothers and Mimi's family. Enveloping each kiss goodbye was the daunting realization that Daniel was moving closer to the unknown war zone. The pain ripping through him let him know that this was as real as real could be.

Departing for the train station, Daniel carried so much more than the single duffel bag he was allowed. He struggled to manage the dramatic emotional mix; family love, elation from celebrating his daughter's birth and his wedding anniversary with the worry for his sick wife and the distress of leaving them for the battle.

Daniel now felt he had been on the train for weeks. The ride to the train station with his sister-in-law, Bea, suddenly seemed so distant. On the way, they were in an accident at the intersection near his sister Rose's house. As the brakes squealed, the car careened onto a nearby lawn. No one was hurt and he reached the train station on time. Daniel briefly pondered the significance, if any, of the accident. Would life be any different if he had been hurt in the accident? Would it only have delayed the inevitable? Then the familiar sound of screeching brakes surrounded him as the train slowed to a halt, and Daniel was brought back to the reality that indeed his duty had not been postponed.

He somberly rose and joined the other soldiers, leaving his seat of memories behind. With a heart much heavier than his baggage, he moved in step with the robotic march of his fellow soldiers to the bus that would take them to Fort Dix, New Jersey. There they would wait with anticipation for their departure overseas.

For the next couple of weeks, Daniel wrote Mimi a few V--mails, letters that were condensed to a very small form. This would be the only time he could communicate with her. There was to be no information on his whereabouts or destination in any correspondence. Although he was relieved to learn that he was not going to the Pacific, he could not share his relief with Mimi because of the censorship.

Daniel knew that he was not going to get home any sooner by prolonging the departure. He was driven to get going, to get it over with, aware that this was the only way back to his family. He could not turn around, he could only go forward. There was no way to avoid the job he was charged to do. Following the army's path into a bloody battle was actually his only way home.

Daniel boarded the Queen Mary with many other courageous, patriotic young men going to battlefields they had never seen, equipped with weapons many had just learned to use. Leaving the shipyard was uneventful. There was no one waving goodbye from the dock because the timing and whereabouts of the deployments were not to be known by others.

The Queen Mary was a nauseating experience for most of the soldiers, with many of them suffering from seasickness. The sleeping quarters were extremely cramped. The bunks, with little space for breathing or moving, were stacked five bunks high. Under these conditions and with unsettled fears, many of the troops did not want to lie down, so, they played poker and black jack throughout the day and night.

There was some discussion about what they would face when they arrived, and where they were headed. They talked about their families, speaking proudly of wives, children, parents, sisters and brothers. Few told the worst stories they had ever heard about the battlefield, while others struggled to find the words to calm the fears of the anxious young men. Of course, what seemed to be a constant diet of fish and chips, did not make the voyage any more tolerable.

The troops were brought to Gurock, Scotland near Glasgow. Daniel's regiment boarded another boat and later beached at Le Havre, France. Then they walked for twelve days through Gervais on the Belgian border into Germany. Their time was consumed by negotiating the terrain, brief stops for K-rations, and more walking.

While walking Daniel stole moments for himself to think about Mimi and Mary Jean; and how much he loved them. At times he tried to imagine where they were and what they were doing. With his heart he prayed for the strength, protection and well-being for his family, himself and his fellow soldiers.

As they walked for days at a time, the soldiers were told that they were ordered to take the Hüertgen Forest in Germany and then advance to the city of Aachen. Unbeknownst to them, similar orders had been given to thousands of soldiers before them. None of whom had ever been trained for forest fighting. These were the orders received by division after division who did not leave the forest alive. Daniel and the other soldiers did not receive any information on what had gone before them.

The Battle for the Hüertgen Forest began on September 19, 1944 with the 3rd Armored Division and the 9th Infantry Division entering the forest. After losing eighty percent of the troops on the front line, those in charge responded to the pleas to 'call it off' by ordering more attacks. The 28th Infantry Division described it as "walking into hell." After two weeks of fighting, all of the officers in the rifle companies had been killed or wounded. With the reported number of casualties between November 2nd and November 13th, 1944, it was evident that every front line soldier was either debilitated or killed, and the 28th Division had essentially been wiped out. (Herr, 2006)

After almost two weeks of walking and with nowhere else to go, Daniel and the U.S. Army, 4th Infantry, 12th Regiment, Charlie Company were the next replacements for the 28th

Division. Upon entering the Hüertgen Forest in November, 1944, Daniel and his fellow soldiers quickly came to know that it was a forest and a fight unlike any other.

"However, Generals Bradley and Hodges remained determined to take the Hüertgen Forest. Having eliminated the 28th Division, they put in the 4th Infantry Division. This division had led the way onto Utah Beach on June 6th, and had gone through a score of battles since. Not many D-Day veterans were still with the division — most were dead or badly wounded. Here in the Hüertgen Forest, the 4th Infantry Division would be asked to pour out its lifeblood again." (Herr, 2006)

Pfc. Daniel Anthony Farchione

Salvatore (1890-1953)
and Sara (1893-1973) Farchione

*Daniel and Mimi Farchione walking down aisle at
St. Mary's Church in Canandaigua, NY Oct. 17, 1942*

Mr. and Mrs. Daniel Farchione walking out of St. Mary's Church, Canandaigua, NY October 17, 1942

Postcard Daniel sent to Mimi from basic training, Summer 1944, back of card

Chapter 2
Fighting the Unknown

Daniel and his company soon realized that to call the Hüertgen Forest a nightmare was a drastic understatement. As they were about to enter the battlefield, they were told that Adolf Hitler had strategically designed the Hüertgen Forest specifically for Germany in war. With this, they now heard that they were replenishing the many divisions that had already been lost in this battle. There were no superior officers, no generals, colonels or captains. Lieutenants would receive radio orders from the other officers located a safe distant from the forest, directing the action from maps. As soldier after soldier was lost, the superiors would radio the command to fight on, continually sending in more men to replace the scores who had already died in this Green Hell Forest. (Whiting, 2000)

Daniel was plunged into battle. The sight, sound, smell, taste and feeling of war engulfed him. Reflections of trees being blown apart lit up his eyes, while bullet after bullet whizzed by his ears. Seeing soldier after soldier picked off by exploding fire power coming from what seemed like all directions turned his insides over and over. He was now completely immersed in the long dreaded fight for his country — fight for his life.

Daniel found himself in a cold, dark forest, maneuvering

through wet leaves, downed trees and fallen soldiers with the need to be highly vigilant for buried explosives. The unusually rough terrain and bitter weather was coupled with almost constant and unpredictable enemy attack. Explosion after explosion surrounded them.

Daniel and the company were completely unprepared for the debilitating conditions. Basic training did not foretell the rigorous conditions of this forest fighting. At Camp Croft, in Spartenburg, North Carolina, they were trained in city fighting and sharpshooting. Throughout the days spent on bivouac, simulating the battlefield, there was not any information on forest fighting. Much of their time was spent in drills on hand-to-hand combat with rifles that were designed with bayonets on the end. There Daniel had received the Expert Rifleman Badge. Even during the time at Fort Mead, Maryland where he received intensive chemical warfare training, there was never a mention of anything like these formidable circumstances.

As difficult as basic training and bivouac were, they did not come close to what Daniel was actually encountering. Here he did not have time to dig foxholes, unlike the well-prepared and well-hidden Germans. The strategies and techniques learned for battlefields and city buildings actually heightened the danger in this setting.

The enemy relied on the poor tactics and inadequate preparation of the United States military. The maneuvers such as air strikes that gave the Americans strength were not possible in the forest. The Germans had tanks. The Americans were mostly on foot and out of their element.

The Germans had set many landmines. In addition, they had created roadblocks of felled, interlocking trees with thick brush, wiring them as booby traps. From bunkers and foxholes, they had pre-set weaponry, ready for the first sign of advancing troops. When they heard the solders attempting to clear the roadblock, they fired from a distance.

The Charlie Company was divided into platoons after entering the forest. Now, Daniel and the soldiers he was assigned to fight with confronted the hurdles for survival. Given the variations in weather and terrain; while attempting to circumvent fiery branches, falling trees, booby traps, rain of hot shrapnel, sniper fire, carnage and the well-hidden enemy, the conditions of this forest battle appeared insurmountable.

The sight of fallen soldiers was sickening. There was no place where Daniel could turn his eyes to avoid the unbelievable scenes. In every direction there was always another horrific sight. With each glance of a lost soldier, the images of his own fate in the forest came flooding in.

As the battle intensified, Daniel never knew from what direction the enemy was going to attack next. The rough forest echoed blast after blast, fiery explosion after fiery explosion, making it impossible to determine the location of the shooters. Aiming his weapon was liking firing at ghosts; uncertain if he was aiming at the source of the fire or simply into the bouncing sound waves.

The German artillery was specially designed to explode as it hit the trees. This strategy sent flaming treetops and branches crashing down on those soldiers who hit the ground as they had been trained. Now Daniel realized even more, that that basic training was practically useless. The closest to "finding cover" was standing up straight against a tree, with the helmet being the only protection from the fire shower.

Even this stance put them in great danger of the mortar fire coming from what seemed like all directions. The ground on which they stood was treacherous with landmines. They were completely surrounded. The enemy was in front and back, beside, above and beneath… day and night. One wrong move in any direction meant a ghastly death.

There was never time for any real sleep. In constant danger, Daniel and his company were continually on the move just to stay alive. With the terrain of the forest, they had to crouch or crawl most of the time, always being challenged by their backpacks catching on trees or the brush. Being on an inch of safe ground at any given moment was a miracle in itself. Getting some rest turned into leaning against a tree, and even that held danger.

Daniel knew that he could not allow fear to paralyze him.

The intensity of the incessant fighting demanded that he overcome the fear with every breath. He would not even have a chance if he did not conquer the thoughts of what could happen. He could not lose focus on defending himself, his fellow GI's, his family and country.

Three days after landing, the reality of war stung in Daniel's heart like never before. Trekking cautiously through the forest, his eyes diligently searched for any movement, any sign of the enemy. Daniel caught the glance of a buddy who was in basic training with him. They had met up with each other again on the Queen Mary. As their eyes connected, they shared the knowledge that the eerie stillness was telling of the impending eruption.

The foreboding of what was to come was increasingly palpable. They continued to quietly study their surroundings, searching for any indication of the whereabouts of the enemy. Then, as it had so many times before, mortar fire crashed through the hush of the forest. More explosions and cries, death once again seized the air.

Daniel swiftly sought to establish some kind of position while trying to see where the fire power was coming from. At the same time, he knew all too well that he could hit a landmine with any given step.

Suddenly, he felt compelled to look out for his buddy. Intuitively, he turned his head, and his heart screamed out in agony. He saw a figure slumped over a tree stump, motionless, fifteen or twenty yards from him. Daniel's heart ached as he struggled to catch his breath. He could not be sure who it was but it looked like his friend.

He wanted to run to him, pick him up, and find him medical attention. He wished for him to get back to his family. The orders to keep shooting and start moving interrupted Daniel's thoughts. He knew that could have been him, and still could be at any moment. He was powerless to do anything. It was clear that the soldier was gone. He hoped that it was not really his buddy. He made a quick but fervent prayer for the soldier's peaceful rest with God and for his family, and then Daniel cried out to God for himself and the rest of his platoon. He never saw his friend again.

Sharing stories with this fellow soldier had been the closest thing to having family around. He felt like this man had known his family. He was a comforting face on the Queen Mary as they had sailed into the unknown. This soldier felt familiar, like a part of home, and Daniel would never see him again.

He hardly knew the other soldiers he was fighting with on a daily basis. They rarely called each other by name. An unspoken rule cautioned against getting too close to each other, for the loss would be that much greater. The rule did not work. Losing comrades one by one, watching reflections of yourself blown to pieces just a few feet away, invited in the unrelenting heartache of losing brother after brother.

Daniel's platoon, now shrunken to the size of a squad, remained on the go. Circumspectly trudging and crawling through the dark, slushy, bitterly frigid forest, encumbered by frequent snow and sleet, the enemy sniped at them from all directions. Never did they receive relief from the fight. A dry spot could not be found. Clothes were wet. Boots and socks remained drenched. Feet were especially freezing causing many to suffer from trench foot.

The Quartermaster Corps was to follow the soldiers with food, water and supplies, but they were not able to get through the forest to the troops. The lucky wounded soldiers received medical attention, some hot meals and coffee at the field hospitals before being sent back into the forest. Daniel's platoon never stopped at a field hospital. He had only heard that these sanctuaries existed. He remained on the battlefield, without a respite stop anywhere, surviving on what little K-rations they carried with them.

There was a medic with them giving medical attention when possible. Daniel was often struck with the vulnerability and courage of the medic. They could lose him just as quickly as any other soldier. Who would take care of the doc? What would they do? On many occasions, Daniel was impressed with the medic's bravery in rushing to the direly wounded. He attended to them swiftly and diligently, despite some apparently hopeless situations. The medic was selfless, assiduously working to bring some comfort in the cruelness of the forest — to save lives and limbs.

The Germans had erected pointed cement structures they called "Dragon's Teeth" forming a barricade for the Hüertgen Forest. They were intended to prevent American tanks and vehicles from entering the forest, and they proved very effective. German tanks however, were in full force, coming from what appeared to be every direction. Daniel and his company continued to move forward on foot, armed with rifles, and a very small supply of ammunition and weapons. Having been targeted by artillery, mortars, and German 88's from enemy pillboxes and tanks, they were especially short on grenades, which continually left them at a terrible disadvantage.

It was Thanksgiving Day when Daniel's platoon stopped briefly to eat their "Thanksgiving Dinner," knowing all the while that they would need to move on quickly. They were pleasantly surprised to find turkey in their K-rations. Despite being a far cry from Mimi's cooking, Daniel was thankful for what little taste the rations offered, briefly refreshing his senses. The dirt and war vapors had pervaded his taste buds. As he was savoring the holiday "treats" in the K-rations, they came to what appeared to be an open space. These clearings were rare. Observing the area, there was a sense of hope that they might actually make it through the forest.

With adrenalin rising, Daniel moved to enter the clearing, aware of the intensifying energy. The hovering trees were no longer closing in. Is it possible that this seemingly endless nightmare through the forest could be almost over? Did they actually survive?

Then Daniel's heart tightened, his gut wrenched beyond what he had ever known. What could he have been thinking? Of course the Germans were not going to leave this clearing undefended. Here is where they would intensify their guard. The Germans had woven foxholes throughout the illusory clearing. No, this was far from a safe clearing. The moment of relief and inner celebration abruptly turned into an ardent attempt to survive beyond the foxholes.

As the soldiers quickly assessed the foxholes, they knew that they were not going to be able to take the clearing on their own. The pounding of their hearts moved through their eyes as they communicated the consternation of yet another intense battle that was sure to ensue. The lieutenant hastily transmitted the enemy's location on his walkie-talkie knowing that they were in desperate need of assistance. He made a deadly mistake.

When calling in the coordinates the lieutenant pinpointed the location of his own squad. Help was so close that it arrived within seconds. Instantly, mortar fire from the American assistance targeted them. The American attack simultaneously detonated the foxholes, spewing German fire. Just as they thought they were coming out of the terror zone, Daniel and the others had actually gone deeper, being bombarded by the enemy as well as their own.

Pure hell again eradicated the silence of the clearing. Booming blast upon blast lit up the sky. Thunderous eruptions vibrated throughout Daniel's body. It all happened so quickly. Complete pandemonium broke loose with screaming, shrieking cries, roaring bursts, fiery debris, hot shrapnel pouring down and the repugnant smell of burning flesh. The earth was convulsing.

Suddenly Daniel felt a burning in his back and a stinging, searing sensation in his left arm. Struggling to stay in the fight, he heard yells for the medic. Before he knew what was happening, he was lying on the ground with the medic speedily working on his back where he had been hit by shrapnel. The medic was selflessly focused on taking care of Daniel despite being in the midst of danger.

When he was finished with the back, the medic turned him over to work on his arm where a bullet had pierced. The medic diligently kept him talking and alert. Abruptly, with an ominous deafening boom, their world was shattered. A mortar shell landed near by. All at once a violent pain imploded in Daniel's back and he was looking into the medic's horrified eyes. In that instant he saw shrapnel ripping through the medic, his guts landing on the ground between them. Daniel plunged into complete unawareness — no sense of existence, no sense of life, a loss of all feeling — silence and darkness.

The next thing he knew he was being kicked and hit, startling him back from the unconscious respite. Dazed, he opened his eyes to see that the violent impacts were coming from a mud-caked boot. Someone jerked him by the arm with great force. He kept hearing, "Mach schnell, mach schnell!" He did not understand the words. He was bewildered and wondered whether he was dreaming, drifting from one nightmare to another. Was it all really happening? He was sharply yanked again by the arm to stand up.

Coming to, he found himself looking into the hardened, bone-chilling eyes of a German soldier. Daniel's insides plummeted into a deep, dark pit, engulfed in stinging, burning pain. All he could think about was that this was the end and that he would never see his family again. He staggered as he was pushed to walk.

Convinced that death would come at any moment, he was surprised the German soldier did not shoot him instantly. This in itself was a miracle, as the Germans had killed many others upon capture. Daniel knew that God's angels were with him. That was all he knew for sure. He did not know what the enemy was going to do with him. He did not know where he was, where he was going or what they were saying.

Again, he found himself walking and walking, another seemingly endless walk. This time he was carrying the residuals of war, pounding, pulsating through every fiber of his being: mind, heart, body and spirit. Without his fellow soldiers, in front or behind him, he was now completely alone in the fight. Memories of the horrible stories of torture flashed through his mind. Daniel was keenly aware that this German soldier could do just about anything with him. He wondered if he would ever eat again, if he would ever see another day. He did not know if he was going to a concentration camp, or if he was going to be shot while walking.

As Daniel continued to walk, the brutal pain in his arm and back, the grueling hunger, and the silent terror within brought him to the frontlines of a new battle for survival. So many times he wanted to collapse, to stop walking, to stifle the agonizing feelings, to stop worrying about what was going to happen to him, and what it would do to his wife, his child and his parents. How and when would they hear? How would they react? The heavy beating of his heart was almost deafening, shutting out everything around him. The darkness pushed to take over. With crushing urges to collapse, he wanted to stop putting one foot in front of the other, to stop taking in a breath, for the breath to stop bringing in life.

Welling up from within his heart, Daniel suddenly saw an image of his beautiful wife, Mimi, smiling and holding their daughter in her arms. Recalling Mary Jean's tiny sweet face, his throat tightened. He reflected on Mimi's courage and stamina during the difficult birth of their child, and offered silent thanks, remembering how close he had come to losing both of them. He also imagined Mimi working in the hairstyling studio. Instead of being defeated by helplessness and loneliness when he was drafted, she had shown remarkable perseverance and ingenuity. Daniel took another breath and moved another foot forward.

In another corner of his heart was the memory of riding in the car with his father on the way to the highway construction job. His father, Salvatore Farchione, had braved the unknown seas in search of a better life in America that he knew was possible. Salvatore was the wise one who highway engineers would consult with. He would bring Daniel to work with him to help and learn at the same time.

One day Daniel and his father were in a car accident on the way to work. They were able to get out of the car and got a ride to work. When co-workers, who had passed Salvatore's wrecked car on their way to work, arrived at the job, they were filled with fear and grief in anticipation of the worst. From the sight of the wrecked car, they seriously questioned the possibility that Salvatore and his son had survived. They were in disbelief when they saw Salvatore and Daniel working.

Salvatore was a compassionate, strong, generous man. He not only gave his wisdom and ingenuity freely without expectation, he also gave of his time and physical labor. He would frequently say, "Hard work never kills you." He often spent his leisure time building homes for others without charge. Daniel was then able to move another muscle, drawing in another breath. Inspired by his father's prowess, Daniel's muscles moved to bring in another breath; taking another step forward.

In another corner of his heart, Daniel remembered his mother, Sara, a generous, nurturing spirit, making food to feed whoever was in need. With the offer of food came also an incredible spirit of giving, for if anyone was in need of money, she would readily go into her special drawer and pull out what she had available and give without question.

With these memories he felt his throat constricting again. He remembered how hard his parents worked for their children. The image of his mother, who was resourceful in her use of all kinds of material to make clothes, tugged at his heart. Given impetus, reflecting on his mother's fortitude, Daniel's muscles moved to bring in another breath; taking a step forward once again.

Reminders of the depth and power of his family's faith, love, and wisdom, united with the same spirit that lived within him. Cognizant that he needed to stay focused on the Lord and his family to keep going, he continued to put one foot in front of the other. Walking in his faith, Daniel accessed the sustenance he needed to overcome all that was attempting to defeat him.

Daniel was taken from farmhouse to farmhouse, and passed from guard to guard. He was interrogated at the first farmhouse without being subjected to instruments of physical pain. Yet, the cruel and inhumane treatment from unintelligible soldiers, holding him at gunpoint was torture. He was continually aware of what the enemy was capable of doing and what they had done to so many others.

They took the gold watch that Mimi had given him. They attempted to take his wedding ring but his fingers were so swollen that they were unable get it off. When they gave up tugging at the ring, he could not understand their conversation. He quaked with the thought that they may be discussing cutting off his finger to get to the ring. Flashes of stories he had heard rumbled through his mind. Germans were notorious for pulling teeth to get a gold filling. They would rather kill than bother to keep prisoners alive. The anticipation of what could happen was tormenting.

Weak, wet, freezing, starving, wounded and traumatized, Daniel was extraordinarily debilitated. Still, he was able to keep breathing and moving. His strength under these circumstances seemed humanly impossible. Walking and walking, deprived of basic human needs, God was carrying him. He was also empowered by his family's love for him — he could feel it.

Mimi often felt Daniel's love, as well as what he was going through. On that cold, dreary November day when he was captured, she was especially sensing him. Sitting at the family table, she had an inexplicable premonition that something was terribly wrong.

Despite the growing discomfort in her stomach, she tried to force herself to eat. Encouraged by family to get the necessary nourishment, her insides tightened. The sight of the food sickened her. The consuming heartache imploded within her core, and the tears burst forth uncontrollably. Being unable to speak, she could not give any kind of explanation for the drastic emotional outburst.

She knew none. All she knew was that something was horribly wrong. There were no words for the agonizing sensations. Other family members were called in to calm her. It was to no avail. The inner turmoil drowned out their words. Mimi was only able to weep.

She had not heard from Daniel since the four V--mails that arrived the first four days of November. These letters were condensed to a very small form by the army and Daniel had been limited in what he was able to tell her. Although he still had not given her the destination, Mimi guessed that he was being deployed to an overseas battle. She did not have any indication what part of the globe he was fighting in, only her fantasies of where and what.

Yet now on this day, there was a deep knowing, shaking her from head to toe; Daniel was not safe. She was able to feel the depths of his pain, agony and despair — the hell that he was living in. Despite their separation, Daniel and Mimi's hearts had found a way to touch, to embrace each other and communicate beyond time and distance.

"Between November 7 and December 3, the 4th Division lost over 7000 men, or about ten per company per day. Replacements flowed in to compensate for the losses but the Hüertgen's voracious appetite for casualties was greater than the army's ability to provide new troops." Lieutenant Wilson recorded his company's losses at 167 percent for enlisted men. "We had started with a full company of about 162 men and had lost about 287." .... After the 4th Division was expended, the First Army put its 8th Infantry into the attack." (Herr, 2006)

Chapter 3

Transcending Captivity: Faith, Love and Miracles

At one point during his forced journey, as Daniel passed an apple tree, his mind's eye caught a glimpse of Mimi peeling apples to make one of her delicious pies. Oh, to have a piece of her pie and a cup of coffee. Heaven on earth! Daniel's imagination brought a fleeting moment of relief. He reached out to pluck an apple. Even though he noticed it was rotten, he was desperate for nourishment. Before he got close enough to touch the apple, the guard yelled and gestured for him to get away from the apple. It was the closest he came to eating food on this journey to the unknown. Continuing the walk at gunpoint, Daniel was utterly exhausted. Death could be upon him at any moment.

Without any idea of where he was or where he was going, Daniel was commanded to get into a German military vehicle. All-consuming dread raged within him as he thought about what was next. Harrowing thoughts of concentration camps with thousands of civilians and soldiers forced to sites of mass destruction plagued him. As horrendous as it was, Daniel found some relief when he arrived at a prison camp instead of a concentration camp. There was a glimmer of hope that he might actually survive. The prison camp consisted of two parts, a prison hospital and the barracks. Daniel was brought to the prison hospital where two prisoners of war, a Russian pre-med student and a French priest, were treating the wounded.

Daniel learned that he had been brought to Stalag 6G near Siegburg and Bonn, Germany. The prison sickbay was purposely located in the St. Benedictine monastery that had been seized by the SS troops. This abbey served as a hideout safe house for these Storm Troopers, considered Hitler's elite troops, who were headquartered here. They were known to be the most heartless, savage German soldiers whose unyielding path was feared by all.

A big red cross on the roof marked the monastery as a neutral bomb-free zone. Next to the prison hospital was a base for V-1 flying bombs, or "buzz bombs," which served as a launch pad for attacks on England. Once they discovered its location, American and English fighter planes tried to knock it out, but were unable due to its proximity to the prison hospital. It was a hospital without medication, clean bandages, or sterile surgical tools. Yet, it housed patients; very sick and wounded prisoners of war.

Shortly after Daniel's arrival, Moose, a prisoner and designated barrack chief from Brooklyn, consulted on Daniel's medical condition with the Russian pre-med student. In addition to the bullet in his arm, there was troublesome shrapnel in his back near his shoulder blade. The biggest concern was his arm, where the swelling and discoloration was steadily becoming worse. When he was first brought in, swollen fingers covered most of his wedding ring. Now, it was clear that gangrene was starting to set in.

Listening to their conversation, Daniel could not and did not want to believe what he was hearing. The swelling was cause for grave concern. If it did not improve soon, they would have to take his arm off. The words shot through him like another bomb. The thought of never embracing his wife or holding his child in his two good arms again was unbearable. How could this be happening?

Daniel was not only unable to wake up from this war

nightmare, he was spiraling deeper and deeper into an endless dark pit of horror. The next night Moose came to Daniel and said, "Farchione, showers for you in the morning." Daniel asked if he was finally going to be able to take a shower. Moose quickly conveyed the reality of the situation. The showers were not for showers. This is where they amputated the diseased limbs. It was time for his arm to come off.

Images of the blood-filled showers made his stomach churn. He had heard the screams and cries of soldiers losing parts of themselves, cutting to his core. How could anyone survive the pain? Especially with the dull makeshift tools they were forced to use for nothing else was available. There was no anesthetic for the pain or medication to prevent infection. He found it hard to believe that this was really happening. It could not be real. He begged and pleaded in his mind, "Please, dear God, do not let this happen to me!"

Daniel felt trapped, helpless. There was nothing he could do. Daniel's life, his very existence was in the hands of these strangers. With nerve-racking images of the bloody showers and deficient instruments cutting through his arm, he wanted to jump out of his skin. There was nowhere to run and even if there was, he was not physically capable of walking more than a few feet.

With the wisdom of faith stirring within him, he was enlightened again with the power of prayer. He wondered about the whole ordeal leading to the prison camp. The fact that he was still alive illustrated the Supernatural Presence was greater than the war, greater than the gangrene, greater than the enemy or the fellow prisoners who made the decisions about his arm. Daniel again tuned into his only hope. He began fervent prayer to God for his arm and his life.

Daniel stayed awake all night praying the rosary. Memories of his life with family and friends drifted through his mind, touching his heart, as he lay asking God to spare his arm — his life. He was aware of the terror that skulked in the spaces between the memories, hovering, ready to barrage him at any shift in focus. He fought to keep his mind and his heart centered on prayer and family.

He remembered when he was he was as a child how excited he was when he figured out a way to bring water up from the canal to the garden. He was responsible for watering the garden daily, which was often a boring and tiresome job. He turned a hose into a siphon and pulled the water up from the canal. He remembered the surprise on his father's face and the twinkle of pride in his eyes when he saw what Daniel had rigged.

What Daniel had considered to be so tedius at that time would have been a party compared to the life he was now leading. Never could he have imagined that he would be lying on a cold, hard bunk without a blanket, across the ocean from his family, in an enemy country, unable to walk without assistance, about to have his arm cut off without sterile surgical tools or anesthesia, by someone who was not a doctor. How he longed to just water the garden again.

Daniel also thought about his mother getting up at 4:00 a.m. on Sundays to prepare the family's Sunday feast. Oh, what he would give for one of her meatballs, homemade gnocchi, baked bread, and fried dough called fritz. She was such a strong, loving mother. He thought of her raising a family, far away from her homeland, and enduring the pain of losing two young children. Daniel reflected on his father's quiet strength. He was a man of few words, but when he did speak, his words carried powerful wisdom. He was a gentle, loving man of integrity, courage and generosity. They were always supportive of each other. They were givers and survivors.

Daniel retreated further to heartfelt memories, envisioning Mimi busy at work in her hair studio. They were financially strained since he needed to leave his job for the army. Expecting their first child, Mimi knew that she needed to do something. She could not sit around and do nothing. With her initiative, she was able to make what was needed to live. She had shown such strength when they had to separate despite the indescribable heartache they were both feeling. She was also a survivor.

The images, impressions and emotions of his life continually flashed throughout the night, bringing Daniel back to the days of peace, fun and the delight of falling in love. He thought of his brother Fred, riding his bike everyday over to their home to help Mimi while Daniel was in basic training. Fred gave up his time with friends to look out for his sister-in-law. He would even stay overnight because he did not want her to be alone.

Daniel's mind replayed the glorious day that God brought him to Mimi's path. Lou, his younger brother, had met her at the Roseland Park Dance Hall in Canandaigua, New York where he had gone with his friend Rocky who had relatives in that small town. When he met Mimi, Lou knew that he needed to introduce her to Daniel. After letting Mimi know about his older brother, they made arrangements to get together the following weekend.

Daniel recalled the day in perfect detail. He was driving his new blue Pontiac Silver Streak to Canandaigua with anticipation and feeling a little jittery. Lou and Rocky, who caddied together, were going over the directions to the cottage that Mimi had given them. She was renting a cottage for the week with her sisters and some girlfriends who worked with her at Newberry's Five and Dime Store.

He had been looking forward to some lakeside fun; now he was wary that the heavy downpours they were driving through might put a damper on their plans. Then when they arrived, they had trouble locating the cottage. Finding the roadways leading to the cottages too muddy, they were forced to give up the search. Daniel drove down East Lake Road, bewildered as to what to do next.

When Daniel saw Crystal Beach, a recreation center, his insides smiled realizing its importance on a rainy Saturday afternoon in a small town. Just moments earlier, Mimi had sensed that Lou and his brother could not find the cottage. With Mimi's encouragement her friends agreed to stop at the beachfront fun spot. Little did Daniel know, he was tuning into his future wife's presence when he pulled into the parking lot.

Daniel recalled seeing Mimi and her friends standing on the porch of the dance hall looking into the parking lot as every car drove in. They strained to see if they recognized the car that Lou had described. Daniel let a little chuckle emerge through the pain as he remembered hearing Mimi's friend enthusiastically announcing that she had found the driver to be a very good looking young man. He smiled with gratitude for Mimi's swiftness. No sooner had Frances finished her declaration than Mimi jumped into the front seat next to him.

He felt warmth in his heart as he recalled the moment that Lou introduced them. He smiled as he remembered her eyes touching his heart, igniting the sensation that he had met the love of his life. He was so sure that he asked her out for the next weekend and confidently brought her to meet his family in Waterloo. Oh! It was so perfect. A dream come true.

Daniel's family and Mimi's family had known each other in Italy, living within three miles of each other in Abruzzi Province. Each had mutual friends in Waterloo, whom they would both visit on occasion, but they had never run into each other. Of course, not until this meeting that seemed to have been divinely orchestrated. Daniel and Mimi often spoke of how dreamlike their meeting was, almost perfection.

Both were so pleased that they spoke Italian fluently and could easily communicate with each other's parents. They both had large families. Mimi was one of nine children, while Daniel had five brothers and sisters. Frequent family gatherings were highly valued and enjoyed by them both. Daniel could not help but wonder what God's plan was if to only bring them together in such a way for such a short time. He had to believe that God had something more in store for their life together, rather than to have it end so quickly in this horror.

Then all at once the silent scream interrupted his inner movie, jolting him back to the reality that surrounded him. The scream reactivated the agonizing sense of impending doom that he had worked so hard to overcome. He had never imagined that on the day he asked Mimi to spend the rest of her life with him that he would be so close to having his life cut short.

When would he wake up from this bad dream, this total nightmare? It was impossible to grasp that he was lying wounded in a prison camp hospital in Germany, waiting to have his arm amputated. He thought of his first exposure to the Army when he was in basic training. He wondered how life would be different had he accepted the offer to go to Officer Candidate School. He had declined because he did not want a military career. Now, Daniel wondered if he would even have a future? In his prayers, he cried out louder and louder, longing for the chance to raise a family with Mimi.

Daniel lay there all night, struggling to breathe under the weight of raw emotion. Again and again he reached out for God's mercy, repeating the rosary over and over. Daniel treasured his fingers more and more with each Our Father and Hail Mary, using them as rosary beads, hoping, wishing, praying for a future life…a life without war.

During this time Mimi was back at home with her worry growing heavier and heavier since Thanksgiving. Having a premonition that Daniel was in serious trouble, her tears had flowed throughout that holiday. She frequently found it building within her. She continually yearned to have some kind of contact with him. Each day carried the deepest most agonizing sensation that she had ever experienced.

She remembered thinking that she would never feel more despair than the day her father died. She had just seen him in the hospital. He looked like he was getting better. Upon waking the next morning, hearing that he had died from a ruptured appendix, her world came crashing down.

Even years later, she recalled how lost she felt at that young age of thirteen. Being flooded with sorrow, she felt helpless in her own grief as well as her mother's suffering. Antoinette always dreamt of returning to Italy, with Pieter assuring her that he would take her. It was no longer a possibility. Mimi wanted so much to relieve her mother's anguish. Now, since she had to say goodbye to Daniel, while holding their daughter, Mimi's knowledge of heartache had reached a dramatically different intensity.

Overwhelmed with emotion, she was driven to express her love for him. She would often type letters in the middle of the night. She diligently kept Daniel posted on what was happening at home while sending him cookies and toiletries. Many times it was so late that she was not allowed to have the lights on. Despite the darkness, she continued to type letter after letter. Mimi's heart seemed to brighten the keyboard. It could be said that she learned to type so well by the light of her love.

The radio and newspapers seemed to burst with piercing reports of battles, casualties and conditions of war. Mimi trembled with the news of severely cold weather in Germany. Every time details came in she wondered if that was where Daniel was located, always trying not to fear the worst. Thoughts of him without shelter in the bitter cold impelled her to help him.

After asking her sister, Mary, to teach her how to knit socks, Mimi quickly got to work. Hoping to send him warmth, she made many pairs of wool argyle socks. Desiring to support her husband in any way she could think of, Mimi ardently mailed letters and packages to the given general APO address without ever knowing if he was receiving them, where he was or even if he was still alive.

Everyone else was going about the daily tasks and business of surviving during war time. Everybody did what they had to do, avoiding conversations about the personal fears and despair. It seemed everyone was touched by the war in some way, yet few, if any, spoke of it.

Mimi had to be strong for their daughter and her family, and most of all for Daniel. With a baby who needed her, she could not succumb to the fear and loneliness. Caring for Daniel as much as she could, despite the distance and unknown, she kept the letters and care packages moving.

On opposite sides of the world, Daniel and Mimi's love gave them extraordinary stamina, binding them with an undying loyalty for each other. Staying focused on each other in mind, heart and spirit, allowed them to unite beyond time and space. They built a transcendent bridge joining them together in the quest to preserve Daniel's arm and life.

While Daniel lay absorbed in prayer and memories, distant voices moved into his awareness. For a moment, he struggled to orient himself, then realized he was hearing Moose and the Russian. He remembered. "Oh! Dear God," his turbulent insides called out. He did not want to open his eyes or let time progress forward in any way. As he listened he noticed the voices were familiar and yet different in some way. They did not have the usual deep sorrow and fear. Voices full of surprise and exclamations of enthusiastic disbelief swirled through Daniel's ears. His eyes popped open, seeking to comprehend the transformation. He was in the same place that he had been the night before. He certainly was not home, and there they were, the two men who were going to amputate his arm.

Now they looked so different. Expressions that Daniel had not seen in so long radiated from their faces, smiles of surprise, and their eyes were wide in amazement staring at Daniel's arm. Moose started yelling for the Padre. Daniel followed their gaze to see what the excitement was all about. "Oh, dear God! Thank you!" Daniel exclaimed. Not only had the swelling gone down but the black and blue discoloration had also disappeared, and the pain had subsided.

Daniel had been graced with another miracle, and how wonderful it was! Unbelievable! Unbelievable? No. How divinely believable! News of God revealing His presence through the miraculous healing of Daniel's arm spread through the prison hospital. This miracle provided some nourishing relief from the helpless agony that was consuming the POWs.

Two days later, the Russian pre-med and the French priest took the bullet out of Daniel's arm. He literally bit a bullet in an attempt to distract from the cutting and digging in his arm while they searched for where the lead had settled. Again, another look of amazement filled the faces of the caregivers. The bullet that they removed was designed to explode upon contact. It was supposed to have shattered his arm. Daniel was struck with such wonder and gratitude for yet another blessing in the midst of the chaos and torment he was living through.

The Padre quietly left the bedside, returning shortly after to give Daniel a Bible. He knew that God had used this wounded soldier to show His presence, and the priest felt blessed to have been witness to these incredible miracles. While Daniel's arm was spared, they were unable to remove the shrapnel from his back, a permanent reminder of the hellish and the miraculous.

About a week after they took the bullet out, Daniel started to get a toothache in a molar. It was infected. Once again, Moose and the Russian medical student consulted and told Daniel that it needed to come out. Adding pain to pain, the tooth had to be extracted without any numbing medication. Since the procedure was being done in his mouth, he could not even bite a bullet.

Just as Daniel thought that he could not bear any more pain... more came. Electrifying, jarring currents of pain shot through him as the prisoners of war turned "dentists" did their best with what they had to get the tooth out. With head to toe reacting to the aggravated nerves, his insides silently cried out for relief. The unadulterated irritation was all consuming.

The conditions in the prison hospital barracks were absolutely terrible. There were not any pillows, conventional mattresses or sheets. The soldiers shared the few blankets given to them. With the latrines outside in the cold, many of the POWs were too sick or weak to get to them. The vomiting, human waste and other smells of sickness and death made the stench putrid.

The dark chill of the prison seeped into every bone in Daniel's body often shaking him at his core. There were no clean clothes. He was still in the same clothes he had on when he walked into the forest. Without adequate water supply, they were unable to shower, brush their teeth, or take care of any basic needs. The POWs yearned for the shower stalls to provide warm, running water instead of the gory remains of the casualties of war.

The prison menu remained the same day after day and consisted of sour cabbage, boiled potato peels and bread made with sawdust instead of flour. The foul odor added to the disgusting taste of the food. In contrast, the aroma from fresh bread that the monks were baking for the SS troops would periodically float through the air from the monastery.

The food given to the POWs was not only repulsive in taste and appearance; there was always the chance that an uninvited creepy crawler would appear in the dish. At the same time, they learned to be watchful of the crawling activity around them. An abundance of mice, ants and cockroaches boldly scampered about without regard for the human occupants.

In the hospital barracks, the POWs could not do anything because most of them were too sick and injured to move. Daniel spent day after day on his bunk, waiting in pain and hunger for someone to assist him in taking a brief walk. He waited in anticipation of impending doom, never knowing how the enemy would decide his fate, hoping for the greatest miracle of all, home.

Laying on the bunk, hour after hour, trying to hide his trembling insides, Daniel's time was spent with the cinema in his mind fighting for attention over the afflictions in his body and heart. He was bombarded with images of fighting in the forest. Internally, he shrieked for those who were left in the forest, bleeding, crying for relief, maimed, mutilated and dead. Daniel was distraught with the helplessness that he felt when he was unable to save his fellow GIs. He was forced to keep moving when his heart and soul wanted nothing more than to reach out to the fallen soldiers that surrounded him.

These memories brought him back to the battlefield over and over again. The vivid scenes elicited mournful thoughts of the soldiers' families; not knowing what had happened to their young men and then realizing their worst fears. They would never see their loved one again.

With a heart beating fierce aches, Daniel desperately worried about what his own family was going through. Worse yet, he wondered had they been told that he was killed in action. Was Mimi thinking that she had to move on with her life without him? He prayed for a way to let Mimi know that he was alive and fighting to survive to return to their life together. He had to get home to his loving wife and daughter.

As Daniel fought the internal battles day after day, laying on the cold, hard pallet, he tried to keep both the prayers and memories in focus. It was his only means of managing.

Trying to make some sense of it all, his mind often went back to the day his world came crashing down. He frequently relived that day when he was driving home from work, looking forward to seeing Mimi's sparkling eyes and contagious smile. He knew that a delectable aroma would greet his senses as he stepped to the doorway of their home. He could almost taste it; like the sweetness of her love. With the nourishing scent filling him, Daniel walked in the door, "Hi, honey! I'm home." There she was busy preparing dinner. Daniel glanced to the counter as he moved toward her for the hug that he had looked forward to all day and every day.

Suddenly, his stomach flip-flopped, his heart started pounding, moving to his head. There "it" was on the kitchen counter. He had let himself forget about it for a minute or two. He knew this dreaded moment was coming, but had avoided the pain of talking about it. He did not want Mimi to know that his deferment would be ending. She had been so relieved that he had a government job that necessitated a deferment. It was a temporary position, but Mimi was comforted in thinking that it was permanent.

He did not want to divert her attention from the joy of preparing for their first child. Daniel's loving enthusiasm for their baby also served as a welcome distraction from the war that was threatening their safe haven. Always aware that his time would come; the inevitable had simply been delayed.

As Mimi turned to him, her arms opened and their eyes met, shocked, stunned with disbelief. No words could be uttered. She recognized the letter. They clung to each other, listening to each other's breath, not wanting to move. They each wished that time would stop at that precise moment. There was not a word to describe the devastation in knowing what this letter meant. Their life would never be the same.

Daniel and Mimi slowly and cautiously released their embrace and looked in each other's eyes. They searched for an answer, for relief from the deepest ache that they had ever felt. This was not how it was supposed to be. This did not fit into the dreaming and planning for their family.

In his heart, he relived that moment when he found out for sure; he would be leaving his family. He realized that he may never see his daughter grow up. With this came the recollection of the emotion rising within him, moving to his throat. "No," he thought, "Mimi must not see my tears. She must only see my courage. I must not upset her." At the same time, he could feel himself holding back the scream, "I don't want to go!" There was no way out, no choice, no alternative.

Daniel called to mind the image of sinking into a chair and Mimi sitting on his lap while they held each other in silence. Listening and appreciating the sound of life, as their breath rhythmically moved in unison with their hearts beating a song of love. Daniel and Mimi's hands moved to her stomach. They cherished their baby together with their hearts' desire for her to know love, safety, security and happiness. They wished and prayed that the last night to hold each other would never come.

Daniel remembered what he had to tell himself to endure the separation and move forward to do what he had to do. He had to protect his family. He could not sit back while the country's freedom was at risk; his family's freedom was at risk. He thought of their parents' courage in coming to this country from Italy. They were so brave to overcome the fear of leaving the familiarity of their native land in search of a better life for their family. They persevered through degradation and persecution as immigrants.

It was his turn to be brave for the love of his family. Daniel's family, his beautiful, lovely wife and child, needed to be safe and secure in a free country, even if it meant giving his life. In serving his country, he was actually serving his family. This was his act of love. There is no greater gift than a man laying down his life in love.

Throughout this time, thoughts of Jesus in His courage and love stirred Daniel. On the day he was called to duty he knew deep within that he needed to summon strength from God. The only way to support his family through it all was to persevere through his faith. He had told Mimi that they needed to pray together, and so they did. Through prayer they were able to experience some relief from the sting.

Daniel remembered the hollow feeling in his gut when the ring from the alarm clock bounced off of the wall the morning of May 19, 1944. It was calling him to the day of goodbyes to those he loved so deeply. How he had dreaded the alarm that morning.

Now, it would be music to his ears.

He longed for any sounds from home as he lay weak, hurting and starving, immersed in the stench and the sounds of the wounded. The pang that he felt that morning in May when his eyes popped open, was a sensation that would intensify and never go away. That day was the beginning of a long journey into a living hell. Daniel realized that as fearful as he felt that morning, it would not come close to the terror of where he was now or what he had experienced. Suddenly, images of the conditions in the forest catapulted him from the warmth of home memories to the grim realities of his life at that moment. More questions stirred within him.

He wondered about the leaders issuing the orders. Did they comprehend the conditions or the situation that they were sending division after division into? How could they order another human being into that hell, especially the young kids, into such a battle without proper training and preparation? He thought of the lieutenant who, in his panic, called in the wrong coordinates. What if…?

Suddenly he was overwhelmed with the glaring truth that no one really knew how to secure victory in this forest battle, not even the lieutenants and certainly none of the higher-ranking officers. There had been no useful training, no experience, no confident strategy, no guidance and no clear objective beyond the daily charge to keep on fighting!

They were so limited in supplies. They were expected to fight without adequate or effective weaponry, or even without dry socks. Socks were a basic essential for protecting their feet, the only means that they had to move forward in battle. How could anyone expect them to be victorious when they were not given critical care and humane treatment? Tragically, for the soldiers from the beginning, they were never given what they needed to wage a successful battle.

Frustrations with the military's expectations and knowing the sufferance due to orders given by those who never even saw the forest haunted Daniel. He thought back on how he and the other soldiers had been talking about the war. As scared as they were, they focused on what they needed to do for their country. They had a job to do. How could they do it under these circumstances?

Daniel and all the other prisoners in the hospital were so sick that they could not move. Making matters worse, Daniel's mind was ensnared by grotesque scenes of fighting in the forest. Helplessness engulfed him. He realized that continuing the war in his mind was dangerously exhausting, putting him at risk to give up. He had to find a way to stop entertaining disastrous imagery. It was vital for survival. He needed every last bit of strength to heal and fight the battle of imprisonment.

Daniel's internal wisdom offered him guidance, leading him to focus on prayer, God's love for him, family love and images of home. He certainly was not going to gain strength from any other source, especially the food.

Days filled with anguish and trepidation moved the soldiers from one holiday to another. They were forced to accept dashed hopes and wishes to be home for Christmas. Daniel could never have imagined that he would spend Christmas in a prison camp. Then again, he never thought that he would be captured; that possibility was never brought up in basic training. Nevertheless, he continued to feel blessed that the prison camp was not guarded by SS troops. Knowing the atrocities committed by the fierce troops, he was grateful that the atmosphere was vastly different.

Though they were not SS troops, some guards were more insolent than others. There were also some Christian German guards who were sympathetic. They allowed the French priest to say Mass on Christmas Eve. The enfeebled voices of the prisoners strained to sing some Christmas carols despite their deteriorated physical condition and emotional exhaustion.

Daniel looked around him. The weak discouraged voices coming from sorrowful, scared faces echoed what he could not put into words. He longed to be home enjoying the festivities with his loved ones. He felt his heart crushing. He was not there for his daughter's first Christmas and Mimi's birthday. It was an extra-special holiday, since it was also the anniversary of their engagement. He reflected on that delightful day when he gave her a watch for Christmas and a diamond ring for her birthday.

He wished he could hold her and let her know just how special she was to him. He thought of the family gatherings. The misery of separation welled within him. There was absolutely nothing to relieve this pain, no anesthesia, no alcohol, no guarantee of freedom. It was raw, pounding, and breathtaking. It stung worse than salt rubbed into an open wound.

The only hope for survival was through God's grace and mercy. He found his focus in faith and motivating memories. He returned to prayer — for a Christmas miracle.

At the same time, Mimi's heart also felt like it was breaking. She could not believe that Daniel was not sharing in Mary Jean's first Christmas. For Mimi, Christmas Eve was the worst day. Mary Jean, who was three months old, was sick and had a slight fever. Mimi was panicked that her child had a fever for the first time, and she was without her husband, feeling very alone. Everyone was going about their usual routine for Christmas. Nobody talked about the emptiness of Daniel not being there.

Mary was sympathetic to what Mimi was going through. She assured her that Mary Jean would be okay. Mimi held her little baby daughter and cried. Rocking her child until she fell asleep, wondering, "Where is Daniel? How is he? How is he spending Christmas Eve? Is he alive? Will he ever come home? Will Mary Jean ever know her father?"

After Christmas, Daniel was transferred to the prison barracks. It was worse than the monastery sickbay, which actually had painted walls. In the barracks there were no showers or toilets, just a spigot with little running water. Lying on bunk beds of improvised mattresses made of straw inside cloth, the wounded soldiers felt discomfort more than rest. The thin wooden walls were unable to keep out the cold.

Many of the POWs, especially the younger ones, refused to eat, which was terribly hard for Daniel to see. He encouraged them to eat, warning them of the dangers of not eating, of starvation and death. He sometimes called them "spoiled brats" in a strategic attempt to get them to eat. Nonetheless, they refused to eat. There were many mornings that Daniel would wake up to find out that another young soldier had died in the night from starvation. They had fought and survived treacherous battlefields but were no longer strong enough to survive the conditions of the prison camp.

When Daniel was thinking about the food, he decided to imagine that he was actually eating it. He realized that as he did this the severe hunger pangs began to ease. Hoping to help the other POWs, he encouraged them to try this visualization. Initially, there was some resistance, but soon some others started to catch on to this strategy.

During the Battle of the Bulge, the huge influx of French, English and Russian soldiers into Germany increased the number of POWs in Daniel's camp — most of them young boys, just eighteen and nineteen years old. Daniel felt a wrenching pang every time he saw a new one coming in. Again and again, Daniel persistently tried to force them to eat. They too refused to eat the junk they were being fed. It was so painful for Daniel to watch.

Among the new prisoners captured during the Battle of the Bulge was Roger, from Green Bay, Wisconsin. He had been shot in the leg. Roger and Daniel quickly became buddies. They shared the same faith and were strengthened by praying together. It was helpful to spend time sharing stories about their families, times past and dreams for the future.

Joe, a teacher from Ilion, New York and Marega, an Italian opera singer and barber, often joined them in their attempts to get through each day. They were able to muster a sense of humor, finding some comfort in moments of joking around. Sports talk was another helpful distraction. This topic frequently evoked a more energized conversation.

Daniel especially liked to talk about the Yankees. He remembered hanging out with friends at the Waterloo newsstand, where everyone went to listen to the Yankees games on the only radio in town that could get the games. Now, Daniel questioned whether he would ever hear another Yankees game. To counter this fear, he enjoyed the banter about favorite teams and best plays. He liked to remind everyone of great baseball moments with Lou Gehrig and Joe DiMaggio. Roger, on the other hand, liked to turn the conversation to tout the Green Bay Packers.

This "support group" spent a lot of time together helping other POWs. Though they were not in the hospital barracks, many of the imprisoned soldiers were both depressed and sick. Most wandered around in a fog, wondering whether they were going to ever make it home. Everyone was petrified and traumatized, fearful of dying or being tortured.

Daniel strongly believed that he needed to hide his trembling insides for it would not be helpful for the others. Roger, Joe, Marega and Daniel were diligent in showing only calmness, doing what they could to distract those around them from the constant sense of impending doom. They tried to console the others who spent most of their time lying around listening to one another cry, moan and scream.

Some soldiers were more interested in talking about what they had just lived through. They told stories of the Germans taking the gold out of their teeth by hitting them with the butt of a rifle. Daniel knew the extremes that the Germans would go to for the gold. While he was thankful that he still had his wedding ring on his finger and that he had never had gold in his teeth, he cringed for the others.

The support group was especially concerned for the young Jewish soldiers who were coming in. They were conscientious in reminding them not to give the Germans their real names. If a prisoner had a Jewish name, they would go to a different camp — a harder camp or something worse. No one ever really knew.

The screaming intensified at night. Marega would sing *Buona Notte, Mama* to bring some comfort in the bitter cold and dreadful aching loneliness of the night. During the day, Roger and Marega provided some comic relief when, Roger, who used to sing in a barber shop quartet, tried to learn how to sing opera in Italian.

Marega also attempted to cut their hair. He soon found it was unsuccessful when he could not rig up a cutting tool that would work. They longed for a hot shower, a good shave, clean, warm clothes, brushed teeth, and food, especially ice cream.

Daniel found that the men in the support group also appreciated the power of imagination. They often wondered how they would get out of this nightmare. When would it be? How would it happen? What would it be like? Sharing their daydreams with each other, mitigated the lonely monotony while reminding them of the power of hope.

At one point, Daniel spontaneously had the idea to prepare a table with a feast. With his words, he carefully created an imaginary spread on a huge non-existent table covered with big steaks, potatoes, green beans, gnocchi, meatballs, apple pie and coffee. He invited the others to join him. There were a few who did. Then, he encouraged the others to partake of the "feast" by playing waiter serving the food.

As time went by a few more prisoners, who were able to use their imaginations, followed the lead. This simple game exercised their minds, strengthened their wills, and gave them a feeling of fullness. Daniel knew that praying, singing, visualizing grand meals, and reminiscing about home and sports provided the strength to keep breathing and keep going.

He was grateful that the guards spared the soldiers more severe treatment. One guard in particular was somewhat friendly and considerate. He was a Christian who had heard of the miraculous healing of Daniel's arm. One day Daniel found the courage to ask him if he could help him get word to his wife that he was a prisoner of war. Worry for his family weighed heavily on him.

Daniel was surprised when the guard brought him a postcard the next day, instructing him to write a brief message. "I am a prisoner of war," was all he was allowed to write. He wanted to say so much more, but he knew that it would be that much more dangerous for everyone involved. He thankfully gave it to the guard with a prayer that it would reach Mimi, and that the guard would be protected from discovery.

Though they had no real sense of time or the number of days that passed, the soldiers learned that Easter was approaching. Lamenting about yet another holiday in captivity, it was clear that they were not going home. Roger and Daniel were inspired to bring the family spirit to the prison camp. Confident in their imagination, they spent their time enacting the home festivities.

They prepared for the family gathering.

While extending the invitation to the others, they set the table. Again, a few would join them. They pictured the family dinner with a big ham, turkey, potatoes, greens, pasta, meatballs, coffee and pie.

The sympathetic guard continued to take risks and show his compassion. On Easter, he brought the prisoners a hard-boiled egg. It was quite a challenge to divide the single egg evenly among all the prisoners. While the situation was deplorable and dark, it was times like these when rays of light would suddenly shine through the hearts of both the captives and the captors.

During their time at camp, the soldiers were kept in the dark about their future. One day the routine changed when guards entered the barracks and ordered everyone to get up and start walking; another march into the unknown. Having no idea where they were going, Daniel thought, "This is the end." He believed they were marching to a concentration camp to be slaughtered.

They moved for days in single file along the Autobahn with German military vehicles buzzing by them. Roger and Daniel continued to fight the inner battles. Now, they were struggling with the fear that they would never see their families again.

Daniel walked and walked with the other POWs through this foreign country, listening to a foreign language, headed for an unknown destination. The only thing he was certain of was his faith. Without food or water, he knew what he had to do for sustenance. However, focusing on hope was becoming increasingly arduous.

Roger stuck right with Daniel. They were able to talk quietly because the guards could not understand English. They discussed the possibility of escaping. Anticipating impending doom, they waited for an opportunity. Looking at each other, a willingness to do whatever they could to avoid execution was communicated through their eyes. What else was there? Believing that they had to do something, the time came.

With a quick, single glance Daniel and Roger gave each other the go ahead and took off. Running as fast as they could into the open field, their fight for survival blinded them to the gross truth of the situation. With Roger's bum leg and Daniel's wounded arm and back, speed was not in their favor. Daniel assisted Roger when he noticed he was lagging behind. The fight for their lives was so compelling that they believed they could escape. All they focused on, all they knew was that they had to run and keep on running.

Within moments Daniel could feel the bullets whizzing by his ear and above his head. The guards were screaming and yelling. Then the thought of being shot and left to die out in this foreign field, left to the buzzards, not knowing when his family would hear of his fate was more than he could bear. With an unspoken agreement, Daniel and Roger turned to surrender. Shockingly, the guards did no more than order the escapees back into the march rather than shoot them on the spot. Was this a miracle or did the Germans want to save Daniel and Roger for something worse?

The POWs walked for days in single file. With every movement came great pain. Consumed with excruciating exhaustion, they could hardly muster enough strength to breathe. When some POWs collapsed, others who were able carried them. Each step brought them deeper into the unknown country, closer to the anticipated concentration camp — or possibly hard labor or even execution.

When they finally arrived, it looked like they had walked to another prison camp. All Daniel and Roger could glean from what the guards were saying was that they had marched to Hofen Stahl, Germany. While the terror of uncertainty still surrounded the POWs, they were relieved that it did not appear to be a slaughter camp.

Daniel immediately noticed the guard tower, a threatening presence that was not at the other camp. This structure defined the magnitude of their oppression and powerlessness. No, they had not been brought to a slaughter camp, but it became clear that this camp was set up to bring them deeper into the hell of deprivation and captivity.

The prisoners quickly learned that the routine would be

different here. Any prisoner who was not wounded was required to go on work detail. Daniel and Roger were spared labor because of their conditions. Daniel felt guilty as he saw those returning barely able to move from debilitating fatigue and hunger. Longing to be helpful, active and outside, he often wished that he could go with the others.

Without the freedom to go outdoors, they were forced to wait for the guards to let them know that it was time for their daily outing. This consisted of stepping outside the door for a very brief and short walk. Back inside, the walls of the barracks felt like they were closing in.

To stay active they would get up, take a few steps, and pass by bunk after bunk only to return to lie down again. The routine was the same throughout the day and night; try to sleep, get up, and walk around a bit and then try to sleep again with periodic requests to use the latrine. Repeated cycles of up and down twenty-four hours and day, seven days a week in the same small, deplorable confined area was their existence.

Although Daniel attempted to build some strength through exercise, he could not do much. He could barely sustain the short walk outside or the trip to the latrine. Home started to become more and more distant while the precariousness of his future loomed large.

Daniel and Roger knew that they had to do whatever they could to prevent the bleak reality from taking complete control of their minds and their lives. The diversion tactics were vital to their survival. With the help of the rest of the support group, they resumed the talks of home and singing as much as possible throughout the day. To help break up the monotony, they made up games, and strongly encouraged others to join them. This brought some relief and gave Daniel some sense of purpose by giving to the others. The talk of sports, especially about the Yankees and the Green Bay Packers, continued to spur some of the more lively chatter. These activities were all they had to help them keep their minds focused, all the while nourishing their hearts and souls.

The food was more scarce here than in the other camp. The

imaginary meals became critical. The soldiers were never sure of when they would be fed. They never received food more than once a day and sometimes days would go by without anything. What little food they did get was like eating garbage. It mostly consisted of the same thrown out potato peels, sawdust bread and sour cabbage.

The mice, ants and cockroaches were at home in this camp also. With the severe deprivation, some of the prisoners wondered about catching the mice or even the cats on the other side of the fence. They discussed that the small wood burning stove providing the little heat in the barracks could possibly be used for cooking. However, being so weak they did no more than talk about it. It was obvious that the animals were stronger and faster, and unsuccessful attempts to catch them would surely be a waste of precious energy.

Daniel was especially hungry for greens. He longed for fresh, green vegetables. He often imagined his mother's greens and beans, but it seemed like a lifetime since he tasted a green vegetable. Temptation faced him when he spotted some greens growing on the other side of the prison camp gate. Memories of picking dandelions under his father's direction drew him to risk moving towards the fence. He could taste home; it was so close and yet so far away.

Sweet images of his mother's delicious dandelion greens with her loving reminders of how good they were for him, drove him closer and closer to the plants. He was just about to grab them when the guard spotted him. The sound of the bullets exploding from the gun, buzzing by his head, riveted Daniel. With flashes of being shot, he quickly jumped back. Instead of killing him, the guard ordered him to get away from the fence. This was yet another miracle. The guard certainly could have justified killing an escaping prisoner.

The feelings of helplessness, combined with the pangs of hunger and the suffering surrounding him, compelled Daniel to do something. He found the despair of those around him to be more and more intolerable with each passing day.

Again feeling driven to try to reach the greens that looked like dandelions, he was determined to not let the guard in the tower stop him. He discovered more on the other side of the fence away from the direct view of the guard. He quietly worked his way towards them.

Daniel could feel his heart pounding, knowing that his life might not be spared if he was caught a second time. Although he was not attempting to get away, the guards knew that he had tried to escape once before. It was the perfect opportunity for the guards to use him as an example for the other POWs. Daniel moved as close to the fence as possible and grabbed a handful of the weeds. Cautiously walking back to the barracks, he worked to contain his enthusiasm, carefully protecting his treasure.

He was so excited to be able to offer his buddies something other than sawdust bread, something that would provide nutrients. He had deep heartfelt hopes that the few leaves would help sustain these kids a little longer, bringing them closer to survival for home. Daniel imagined that the greens were going to taste like his mother's dandelions and that everyone would enjoy them.

Then he remembered that his mother used more than the dandelions to make the dish. Focused on eating a vegetable, Daniel had overlooked that he would need oil to cook the dandelions. One of the prisoners on work detail had found a piece of fat. Daniel and the others stood around the wood burning stove, melting the fat to cook the dandelions. These greens were such a welcome distraction from the dreadful, repulsive food they had been forcing down.

The prisoners eagerly gathered for what looked like a feast. In their determination, they had not considered that their bodies were so deprived of nutrients that their systems might not be able to manage the greens. They soon found out about their sensitivities when they all got very sick. Daniel felt terrible. He had wanted so much to bring some relief from the suffering and now he could not believe what was happening.

He looked around and all he saw was sickness and a dense foulness wreaking the air, stifling each breath. Helplessness and hopelessness weighed heavily on his heart. Through their sickness, the soldiers noticed Daniel feeling miserable with guilt. Knowing his good intentions, they attempted to convince him that they were grateful for his efforts in giving them a taste and the shared camaraderie in preparing their feast.

Dawn and night continued to cycle; the filth and stench building day after day. The prisoners had no recourse but to lay around in scum and vile, with the insects and rodents. Waiting, wondering and scared, they were in a constant state of hunger, hurt and helplessness. The POWs were becoming weaker and weaker by the minute in body and spirit — losing all sense of hope. How would they ever be rescued or set free? Did their families think they had died? Did anyone know where they were? What was happening in the war?

Daniel knew how important it was to be hopeful, but this was becoming so difficult. He remained very much alone with the exhausting, devastating imagery of the Hüertgen Forest. He was the only one in the prison camp who had known this battle.

Sleep brought tiring nightmares of the gruesome forest fight. Dreams of home provided fleeting bliss only to awake to the brutal truth, bringing on more fatigue.

As difficult as it was becoming, Daniel and Roger knew that they needed to stay positive and keep their minds active. Without their imaginations, they would be completely enslaved in the permeating, raw, stinging wretchedness that they were immersed in. Daniel continued to pray for the strength and the way home.

Mimi and Mary Jean Farchione, Portrait Mimi had taken to send Daniel. He never received it.

Prison camp bunks (this is not where Daniel was held captive but it looks the same as his barracks)

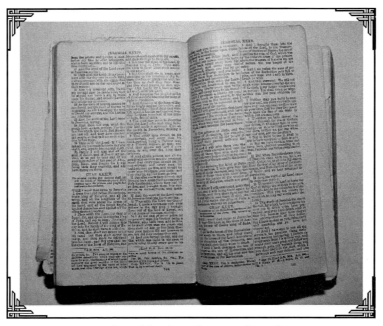

Holy Bible that the French Padre gave to Daniel in prison camp

Chapter 4
Through the Tunnel:
Light of Liberation

Daniel woke with the all too familiar nausea in the pit of his stomach. As his eyes adjusted to the nightmare around him, he wished for his dreams to come alive. He was unsure of what time it was or when he had fallen asleep. Daniel knew that it was daytime and that he had gotten through another restless night. The chow for the day had arrived. Forcing down yet another distasteful meal, he heard someone ask if anyone knew what day it was. They agreed that it was April 12, 1945. Daniel walked around a little and then headed back to the bunk.

Abruptly, the guards hastily commanded all the POWs outside and then ordered them into the trenches. All of a sudden, Daniel was surrounded by dirt, aghast that the long feared execution was imminent. Heart pounding, Daniel clutched the Bible that the Padre had given him. Noticing Roger with a rosary, he reached out, joining him in clinging to the prayer beads. They prayed that it was not as it appeared — the end.

After what seemed like hours later, the guards directed them back to the barracks, conveying that it was an unfounded rousing.

In the portending atmosphere, the guards were harried. The POWs were confused and trepid, not knowing what to expect next. There was cause for alarm.

Suddenly, the guards started scattering in all directions. They were actually running away from the prison camp. Daniel could not believe his eyes. Did he really wake up or was he still sleeping? Some of the POWs pointed in disbelief towards the guard tower. In complete shock, they watched it come crashing down.

Daniel and Roger looked at each other, confused. Within moments they heard a distant roar coming closer and closer. Anticipation filled the air as the POWs dared to hope. Are those American tanks? Could this be real? Are we waking up from the nightmare?

It took a moment to grasp the connection. "Well, of course, they must be Allies, if the tower is coming down!" Daniel thought. Life in slow motion quickly jumped to fast forward. Before Daniel knew it, he was being taken out on a stretcher, looking into the faces of American soldiers and listening to directions in English. It was soothing music to his ears. While he was being loaded on the ambulance, the radio operator was passing on the news as it was coming over the radio, "President Roosevelt just died."

"Who the hell cares?! Just get these boys out of here!" the Major vehemently ordered. Daniel was instantly nourished by the Major's compassionate attention. His top priority at that moment was the well being of the American soldiers. Daniel would never forget his response.

At that same moment, Mimi was in the bedroom with Mary Jean in her crib. It had been a little over a month since she had received the postcard with the message in Daniel's handwriting letting her know that he was a prisoner of war. She distinctly remembered that day in the first week of March, when she noticed a very different expression on the mailman's face as he approached her. He let her know that he had something for her that day. With trembling hands, she clutched what she had been longing for, for so long — some contact from her husband.

The emotion as her eyes caught the words, "I am a prisoner of war," was inexpressible. She read the words over and over, wishing, hoping each time that there would be more information. The questions in her head swirled in rhythm with the rapid beating of her heart. It was a bittersweet moment. For the first time since November, she had a tangible message from her husband, letting her know that he was alive somewhere. Yet, there were many unknowns.

It had never crossed Mimi's mind that he could be captured. She could not even imagine what it meant that he was a prisoner of war. The media reports never said anything about soldiers being held captive. She hadn't heard of anyone being in a prison camp.

The only thing she had heard was that there was an international agreement regarding the treatment of prisoners. From this, she ascertained that he was not being tortured. In fact she thought he might be safer in a prison camp rather than on the battlefield. She realized that she actually did not have any idea what it meant to be a POW. What was happening to him? How would he get home? Mimi listened to the radio in her bedroom whenever possible, hoping to find out more about prisoners of war; and that Daniel would come back to her and their daughter alive and well.

Now, on this April day, while Mary Jean was sleeping, she sat on the bed with the familiar heaviness in her heart. She longed for more information, some glimmer of hope. Contending with imaginings of the worst, she pleaded with God to bring her husband home safely.

Listening to the news, Mimi was taken aback. She could not believe what she was hearing. President Roosevelt had just died. All at once, without any time to digest the staggering news, Mimi was given another shock. Mary Jean pulled herself up in the crib for the first time and then proudly announced that she had found her first word, "DaDa!" How extraordinary! Mimi was amazed. Mary Jean had not seen her Daddy since she was a month old. Yet, it seemed like she was calling out for him.

Mimi wanted to believe that the shift in Mary Jean

signified Daniel's return. Awestruck with her daughter's new developments, she could not have known just how astonishing the timing truly was. The hearts and spirits of a father and child were communicating across the miles, the joyful miracle that her daddy was on his way home.

In the distant prison camp, Daniel was experiencing absolute jubilation! Explosions of a whole different magnitude and emotion burst forth. Shouts of joy, triumphant cheers and cries of exuberant delight cascaded from the lips of the liberated soldiers. "We are going home!"

Daniel felt like a victor winning a championship game. He looked up to heaven with his arms raised and said, "Thank you, God, for answering my prayers!" He was keenly aware of the faith, love and miracles that had brought him through the hell to this glorious resurrection to freedom.

Jostled by the bumps in the road, Daniel's stretcher seemed to bounce him in rhythm with his dancing insides. While riding from the prison camp to the base hospital in Germany, Daniel found himself thinking about his new reality. Freedom. How many times before had he wondered how freedom would actually happen? The sense of hopelessness and powerlessness had seemed so all consuming, that there was no way out, while the comforts of home were so distant. He had survived a constant diet of inhumane living conditions filled with oppression and cruel, harsh treatment.

Finally, after months of longing and agony he was going to be with his wife and daughter. He was going to see his family. The time was coming when he would be able to bathe, shave, brush his teeth, and change into clean, warm clothes. He would soon be smelling and tasting nutritious and delicious food… ice cream, fresh bread, vegetables, pasta, meatballs, strawberries. Simple everyday activities and pleasures that he had once taken for granted were now cause for celebration. He had his life back.

For the first time in months, but what seemed like years, he had some relief from the nagging terror that his life could end at any moment. Yet, a lingering apprehension remained. He prayed he would have a smooth trip home safe from harm's way, and that this was not a dream or illusion.

Laying on the stretcher, being carried into the base field hospital, was like floating on a cloud. Daniel was aware of the people scurrying around him. As much as he had prayed for this moment, this liberation, he had never imagined what he would encounter on the road to freedom. He grappled to comprehend that this was happening to him and those who had been in captivity with him. Welcoming orders then snapped him to attention. "Give them anything they want." Daniel struggled to register the moment. They were talking about him! They were actually prepared to give him anything he wanted.

Much to everyone's surprise the first choice for many of the liberated soldiers was a hot dog! The flavor of the meat was beyond words, and the bread tasted like angel food cake. Yet, Daniel and the others soon found out that their systems reacted the same to the hot dog as to the "greens." It did not make any difference that this was real food. Everyone got sick.

Daniel wanted to get home as soon as possible, but he was very ill. With his wounds not yet completely healed, the shrapnel in his back, physical exhaustion, weight loss and malnourishment, it was a miracle that he was alive at all. He was not about to complain about the time that was needed for him to heal enough to travel home. The doctors decided to transport him across the channel to a base hospital in Marlboro, England.

As he was being carried into the hospital on the stretcher, he took in his new surroundings and heard the rushing of people around him. He heard a cry of disbelief. The voice filling the air was familiar to him, but he could not place it immediately. Then as the voice moved closer, calling his name, he was able to see the face that belonged to the voice. It was Ray, a soldier from Canandaigua, whose assignment was administrative clerk at the base hospital. Ray and Mimi's brother Vic were best friends. Ray had been bringing coffee to another friend, when he spotted Daniel.

Daniel could not believe that he was actually talking to someone who knew his family and his wife's small hometown. Through the dark miles he had walked, and the endless sea of faces of war he had seen, Ray's face was a light shining with hope, revealing a promise for the future. Daniel now believed he was moving forward to the life he had almost lost, the life that he had only lived in his imagination. He took a deep breath, savoring his resurrected existence.

Vic, a second lieutenant in the armored division, was assigned to drive the tanks liberating the prison camps as Germany was taken over. Vic had received a letter from home telling him that his sister had not heard from her husband. Everywhere he went, Vic had Daniel and Mimi on his mind. He he searched at every opportunity, asking if anyone had seen or knew of his brother-in-law.

As Daniel and Ray exchanged greetings, they were both astutely aware that the war was not yet over. Vic was still in the field, courageously moving from prison camp to prison camp. There were so many POWs who were waiting, hoping and longing to hear the roar of American tanks coming to the rescue. Daniel's ears continued to carry the sweet song of freedom coming from those roaring liberation vehicles.

The last stretch of Daniel's journey home was much longer than he would have liked, but he did not complain. It was decided that he needed to take a hospital ship home. Roger, on the other hand, was able to fly home. Daniel was severely malnourished and too sick to fly. Standing at six feet tall, he had dropped to 127 pounds, having lost 73 pounds since leaving for battle. Although Daniel needed to wait longer to be reunited with his family, he was grateful to be under a doctor's care and was well aware of the seriousness of his physical condition. The extra recovery time was greatly needed and gave him an opportunity to adjust to being free again.

The hospital mattress on the ship was like sleeping on a cloud, soothing his exhausted bones and muscles. Daniel felt like a king as the doctors and nurses attended to his care. There were so many nurses, almost one per soldier. The soldiers could get just about anything they asked for except for a cola; although most of them tried very hard to convince the doctors to allow them the soda. Strained baby food became the main course on the menu.

Actually, it was the only thing on the menu for Daniel, but even that took on the quality of gourmet food after the months of starvation.

Daniel especially looked forward to being wheeled out to the deck to enjoy the blue sky and warm, embracing sunshine. Now his dreams of going home were coming true. In anticipation of returning home, his mind was filled with thoughts of reuniting with his wife and daughter. He hoped that Mimi had received his postcard, and that it had helped her. Concerned for his parents, brothers, sisters and in-laws, he was aware that he had no idea what had been going on with any of them during this time. Was everyone still alive and well?

Then he thought about those he cared about with whom he had just been liberated. He wondered about Roger's journey back to his loved ones. Being whisked away when they were rescued, he realized that they did not have time to exchange information for future visits. Roger had become like family to him. They were so much a part of each other's survival. He did not want to think that he would never see his friend again.

Much to Daniel's chagrin, he found his consciousness returning him to the battle and the prison camp. Although he tried to shut out these scenes, the macabre invaded his mind unannounced and uninvited. Daniel's insides cried for the soldiers who were not coming back with him. If only those young kids in prison had eaten what was given to them, for as awful as it was, it was better than nothing. If only they had joined in the imaginary meals ... Daniel was often overcome with grief for them.

The thought of having to tell anyone about his time in the forest wrenched his heart. The relentless war scenes continually reminded him of the dramatic contrast between the two worlds. It was hard to comprehend that he was even on the same planet with other human beings. Daniel concluded that he should spare others the reality of what people in war were doing to each other.

What good could it possibly do to speak of these things? He could not even begin to form the words. These images were going to have to go away, he thought. Surely, when he was able to be with Mimi and Mary Jean every day, he would not have to deal with these memories. He would be too busy making happy, fun memories, raising his family.

Daniel thanked God that this dream was truly real and that the nightmare had finally ended. Unbeknownst to him, this nightmare was not going to disappear so easily. He had lived it. He had experienced it. It was now a part of him. He had no way of knowing how vivid the war would remain in his mind, his heart, and his body and spirit; and the frequency with which he would relive it through the nightmares and flashbacks.

As the Chateau Thierry, a U.S. Army hospital ship, sailed closer to the coveted destination, Daniel was prepared for what was to follow. After they docked, he would be able make a brief call home before leaving for Rhodes Military Hospital in Utica, New York. The medical staff informed him that he would need to be hospitalized for a while but would have weekend passes. He was advised that the initial homecoming pass might not be granted for at least a couple of weeks.

Daniel was simply grateful to be speaking with people who guaranteed that he would be returning to his family. He appreciated being surrounded by people who were able to freely attend to his well-being.

The New York skyline, becoming increasingly visible, was an absolutely spectacular sight to Daniel. Remembering the last stop before departing from his homeland, he was elated to know that he would soon step foot on American soil again. This meant that he was getting closer and closer to the most treasured phone call he ever made. Daniel ecstatically rehearsed the call to Mimi, praying that she would answer on the first ring.

Disembarking from the ship, Daniel's only focus was to get to a phone as quickly as possible. Now, the moment that he had longed for, prayed for had finally arrived. So many times he had dreamt of making this joyful phone call and hearing Mimi's voice. Trying to stay composed, he enthusiastically picked up the phone. He could not get Mimi's phone number out fast enough.

It was May 19, 1945 when Mimi woke well aware of the significance of the date. It was on this day, just one year ago, that

Daniel had left for basic training on the bus from the front of the court house in Waterloo. Dazed and numb, she felt so lost waving goodbye and blowing him kisses. She was thankful for her sensitive and caring mother-in-law who insisted on cooking dinner for her that evening. The devastation, especially when thinking about being alone at night, without him, was beyond words. She felt such gratitude for Fred staying with her to alleviate her worries.

Everything seemed like a blur since the draft notice dropped like a bomb on their cozy, happy life. From that point on, their days were occupied with preparing for his departure. It was hard to believe all that had transpired in just one year; she had a baby, Daniel left for war, and she had not had contact with him for most of the year.

Urging herself to go about her daily routine, the sadness of another day without him; another day of fear and worry weighed on her every move. Mimi's thoughts brought her back to the day she received the postcard back in March. The little relief from the postcard was all but almost gone.

What is he going through? What are they doing to him? Are they feeding him? Is he warm? Could they have killed him in prison camp? She felt like she was going to explode inside as she longed for some sort of reassurance, a guarantee that he would come home. It seemed so long ago since she had experienced that brief moment of joy, the day Mary Jean said her father's name for the first time. She had thought that it had been some small sign of hope, but ever since then, the days continued to grow longer and heavier.

As she had been doing for months, she managed to move through her day despite the emotional burden she carried. She helped her mother while her sisters were at work. Watching her mother, Mimi wondered how she had gone through all these years without her husband. Mimi could not bear the thought that Daniel might not come home. She would not accept that he could be dead, vanished from her life, as her father had disappeared from their lives.

Mimi had become quite the expert on taking care of her day

to day responsibilities while hiding the intense agony and despair she battled every minute. Sometimes family members would ask if she had heard from Daniel, offering reassurances, encouraging her not to worry.

With so many young men gone to war and so many families in pain, that to give in to the emotion would be paralyzing. It was simply expected that everyone would do what had to be done and focus on the tasks at hand. It was a matter of survival.

Mary Jean's cry brought her back to the demands of the moment. She had a part of Daniel right there. She could touch and hold her beautiful daughter who needed her mother's attention. What if she was not able to know her dad and what if Daniel was never able to hold her again? She remembered how close they had both come to dying during Mary Jean's birth.

Mimi's recollections of the vision of Mother Mary brought her a bit of comfort. Although, she rarely spoke of this divine experience, she treasured it deeply in her heart. She was still in awe that it had happened to her. This was a blessed gift that helped her get through these difficult days with more faith and fewer tears. Staying focused on this loving reassurance that God was with her family, she felt hopeful. Mimi held her daughter close to her heart.

Absorbed in her thoughts, she was startled when the phone rang. She always got a sinking feeling whenever the phone rang, never knowing what information was going to come through. She always wondered, if "it" were to happen, whether she would hear by phone or see the car drive up to the house. She had heard so many stories of getting the word, the dreaded message of death in these ways. She felt herself shaking more than usual when she picked up the phone on this day.

When she said hello, her quivering voice revealed an apprehension. The voice that came through the line took her breath away, tears of joy flowed. "Daniel!!!" She was in shock and disbelief. "Is this really you? Is this really happening? How are you? Where are you? When are you coming home?" Mimi felt her heart beating through her skin as she heard him say he was coming home and that she would actually be able to see him. Elation.

She trembled with enthusiasm as she hung up from the brief but blissful phone call. Her head whirled with people to call and all the preparations to make. First and foremost, she had to call Daniel's mother, Sara. She phoned Sara's neighbor, as his mother did not have a phone. She urgently asked for her mother-in-law, being careful to make sure she told Sara first. She could hear the trepidation in Sara's voice, knowing that they all had daily battles with anxiety whenever a phone call came through. Mimi quickly let her know that she had good news. She did not want Sara to bear another second of heartache for her son. Sara joyfully exclaimed, "Gratais Dei!", thanking God in Italian. They hurriedly prepared to share the good news with family and friends.

Upon Daniel's arrival at the hospital, the barrage of medical tests and close monitoring of his diet started immediately. While he needed to gain weight, the doctors also needed to be cautious due to the damage caused by the severe starvation. The medical staff did not, however, deal with the psychological trauma he had endured. Nobody talked about it.

Yet, Daniel continued to silently battle the imagery of the forest, the maimed bodies, and the desperate cries for help. Alone with his memories, the stabbing pain in his heart came forth in waves, eating at his insides. The faces of those who he was unable to help played like an endless movie, igniting the powerless and helpless feelings that he had fought so hard to breathe through.

This inner turmoil was in absolute contrast to what he was seeing around him. Daniel lived in two worlds. He watched the activity in the hospital, the busy nurses taking care of the soldiers, the doctors in and out checking on the physical conditions of the wounded. All the while, his heart trembled with the suffering of war, and a profound awareness of his loneliness with these memories of the Hüertgen Forest and the prison camp. He often heard stories of the Battle of the Bulge floating in and out of conversations around him but not a word about the forest. Did anyone know about the Battle of the Hüertgen Forest? Did anyone else survive?

He was able to call Mimi a few times, and they enthusiastically planned their reunion. They arranged for Mimi to come to Utica on the Saturday before Father's Day. After staying overnight together, they would drive to Waterloo for the reunion with the family.

Driving to Utica, Mimi was still in shock. As much as she had longed for this moment, she found it hard to believe that it was finally happening. She was stunned. It was almost like she was going on a first date rather than a reunion with her husband. She did not know what to expect. She had pictured this moment so many times, wondering what it would be like. Then suddenly, yet at long last, the moment had arrived.

As she walked towards the hospital she saw a very thin soldier running towards her. Focusing, she realized it was Daniel. He had told her that he had lost a lot of weight, but she had not imagined he would be this thin. Before she knew it, they were wrapped in each other's arms with tears of happiness replacing the stinging ache in their hearts. They held each other so tightly, not wanting to ever have to let go again. Words could hardly express what it was like to move from a nightmare to a dream fulfilled, a rapturous reunion after a living hell. After months and months of worry, they were able to see and touch each other. They were going to be able to fall asleep in each other's arms and wake up to each other.

Mimi quickly noticed that Daniel was not wearing the watch that she had given him. With her burning desire to take care of him, she wanted to buy him a new watch right away. This shopping mission was their first activity of the day.

Throughout this precious time, Daniel and Mimi were completely wrapped up together in their own world. Mimi could not wait to hear how he enjoyed all the packages she had sent him. She especially wanted to know whether the socks were helpful and about the portrait she sent of Mary Jean and her. She was sadly surprised that he never received anything.

Realizing that he had not had any news from home, Mimi caught Daniel up on the events since he had left. Daniel showed

Mimi the bullet, the evidence of his miracle. However, he told her very little about his experiences. Mimi sensed that it was too much for him to talk about and knew it was best not to ask questions. She knew that when he was ready, he would talk to her. Instead, Mimi told him stories about Mary Jean growing up, which provided the much needed comfort for Daniel. They were simply enthralled with each other.

On Sunday they headed for Water Street in Waterloo, New York, to the home Daniel grew up in for the reunion with the rest of the family. Riding in the car, holding hands with Mimi, Daniel enjoyed the warm breeze, fragrant air and the sight of her hair blowing in the wind, soothing his eyes. Drinking in the moment, he anticipated greeting his family.

Daniel had replayed visions of this family reunion a million times in his mind. Daydreams of the homecoming became a necessity as they were all he had to distract him from the inundation of flashbacks. Finding that each day brought him back to the war and prison camp, it sometimes seemed that he was only rescued physically.

Upon pulling in the driveway, Daniel's mother rushed out of the house, barely greeting him before ordering them back into the car. With tears in her eyes, she directed them to drive to St. Mary's Church. She opened the front doors of the church, immediately knelt down and proceeded down the long aisle on her knees, giving thanks to God for her son's safe return. It was an incredible sight. Daniel struggled to breathe as his emotions overwhelmed him. This was the immensity of the family's faith and love that he had felt over the miles, strengthening and supporting him throughout his ordeal.

Returning to his parents' home, the sight of smiling faces and the delicious aroma filled him with a dreamlike joy. It seemed so long ago that he had said goodbye to everyone. Daniel felt like he had lived in a whole other lifetime. Flashes of all that had happened in the past tumultuous year became a part of all that was happening in that moment.

Family members eagerly greeted him with enthusiasm. The sight of his weight loss evoked an even greater concern for what Daniel had endured. Sensing his reluctance to talk, they respectfully did not ask about his experiences. They focused on celebrating his return for he had been sorely missed. The family gatherings had not been the same especially without his humor. Now, once again, Daniel's joking ignited the family's togetherness in merriment, enjoying the sweetness of his safe return home.

His father quietly welcomed him home. He did not say much but his eyes spoke of his love, pride and relief. His son was home.

Daniel was delighted to meet his new nephew, Samuel Patrick, the newborn son of his brother and sister-in-law, Patrick and Rose, who was almost three months old. He was thrilled that their dream of having a son was fulfilled. He knew how much his brother wanted a family. He was so proud of his brother's many accomplishments in overcoming his hearing impairment. At the same time, Daniel was sad that he had not been around for his brother during this precious time in his life.

Daniel immersed himself in the delighted faces of his loved ones. He was embraced by the laughter, bringing the much needed healing. Effortlessly returning to the rhythm of the family fun and love, he basked within the comforts of home.

Sara immediately started serving the first course of the seven course feast she had prepared for his homecoming. Since Daniel was still on the baby food diet, he was only able to have small tastes of the meal. Although his mother lovingly wished he could eat much more. He was grateful that that his system could handle at least some of the delicious delights which for so long had only been in his imagination. He had to keep reminding himself that he was not going to wake up from this dreamlike homecoming and find himself back on the hellish battlefield or prison. He was filled from head to toe, from inside out, with joy, love and gratitude. It was a splendid reunion; a true feast of love, laughter and warm homemade bread.

Daniel did not want to distract from the fun and festivities in any way. At the same time, he wondered if his family could possibly comprehend the depths of his appreciation for the smallest comforts, even the discomforts. For nothing, absolutely nothing came close to the never-ending misery of the forest and the prison camp. No one asked and he never told anyone about the living hell he had left behind. He was simply grateful that his loved ones were spared this horror, and that he was given back his life with his family. Daniel knew that he would forever savor the delectable tastes of love and life.

Sara Farchione

*When he returned, Sara took Daniel and Mimi
to St. Mary's Church, Waterloo, NY,*

*Daniel, Mimi and Mary Jean, reunion with family
in Waterloo, June, 1945*

*At family reunion in June, 1945
Waterloo, NY, Daniel's first glimpse of
Mary Jean since he left*

Chapter 5
Post-war:
Life Lessons, Battles and Triumphs

For the first six months after his return, Daniel stayed at Rhodes Military Hospital. He was allowed to go home on the weekends. As difficult as it was in his physical condition, he would hitchhike to their home in Waterloo, and Mimi would drive him back on Monday morning with Mary Jean in her baby seat.

As much as Daniel looked forward to completely engaging in life, he did not foresee the war residuals and social implications that would confront him. The discouragements were often heartbreaking as Daniel noticed not only for himself, but for other veterans, that their time in service was of little value when it came to acquiring profitable employment. He experienced many ups and downs trying to provide for his family. Daniel and Mimi diligently worked long, hard days and nights to ensure that their children had what they needed.

Whatever Daniel was up against through these post-war battles, he moved forward with the same determination that he put forth in taking care of his country and his fellow soldiers. With every life lesson, battle and triumph, he also overcame the continuing fight for survival in the forest and the prison camp. The flashbacks continued to intrude on his day to day life as a result of what he now knows is Post-Traumatic Stress Disorder.

Although Daniel was accomplished at hiding the war scenes occurring in his mind, his nightmares alerted Mimi to the inner distress. Still, he secretly faced these hostile movies throughout his waking hours. Mimi quietly supported him in any way she could, without pressuring him to talk about it; and he never did. She intuitively knew that the nightmares were too painful to speak aloud. Through it all, they continued to support each other. None of the disappointments or obstacles in their life could compare to what they had lived through while being separated from each other.

With unwavering courage, he looked for the lessons within the vicissitudes of life, and his wisdom expanded. He knew what he was capable of enduring, and he knew that adversity could be overcome with diligence and vision. Daniel continued to appreciate every moment of life with unyielding patience and calm. No matter what he encountered, he always knew what could have been. He knew that goals were accomplished through perseverance, courage, focus and love — through the grace of God.

He found more traditional jobs physically and emotionally uncomfortable. Confinement in a work place was very difficult, triggering sensations of prison camp. Daniel's severe back pain was often disabling; however, he was determined to not let it immobilize him. He gravitated to positions where he did not feel hemmed in, that allowed him freedom of movement.

Daniel never stopped appreciating life or every pleasing taste of fresh food. He continues to have an apple, if not two, each day and savors every bite, just as he relishes every meatball, gnocchi, fritz, greens and beans, fruit salad, soup, strawberry shortcake, fresh bread and ice cream. Of course after every meal he gives thanks, often declaring, "There's nothing like a fresh cup of coffee and warm apple pie." He always ensures that food is not wasted. Daniel consistently expresses his gratitude, no matter what life may bring him.

For Daniel, his greatest treasure is certainly his family. "Five daughters and finally a son" was a popular greeting the family received. Though there was quite a bit of teasing revolving around the raising of five girls and their perseverance to have a son, Daniel always conveyed pride in all of his children. Most importantly, he is tremendously grateful for the enduring love of his precious family, his beautiful and loving wife and his six children: Mary Jean, Joanne, Linda, Donna, Sharon and Daniel, Jr.

Daniel's creative mind certainly played a major part in his survival. These gifts were with him throughout his life from childhood through the battles and prison camp, to his post-war life. From siphoning water for the garden and as the art editor for his high school yearbook, to creating diversions for survival and onward, Daniel's creative ideas continued to surge through him. These visions encompassed innovative ways to improve the quality of life.

Within Daniel's choices for employment throughout the years, there was a desire to be helpful to others. Shortly after his return home, Daniel was considering entering into the real estate business, when he was offered an attractive opportunity to manage a soda shop in Canandaigua. This was bittersweet because he was looking forward to pursuing a career in real estate. With the offer came the deciding influence for Daniel, he was truly needed to help this business succeed.

He was soon managing the Hi-Lite Soda Shop, taking great pride in creating a memorable place to eat. Not only was the delicious food an attraction, but Daniel's personality was cause for many to return for the warm, family atmosphere he instilled. While providing nourishment for the body, he also fed the minds, hearts and spirits with care, respect and appreciation. There was always great, genuine conversation filling the air. Daniel was again surrounded by young people seeking supportive, helpful and fun conversation that could always be found in this small town eatery. These teenagers enjoyed the welcoming and comforting environment that he had created.

Later Daniel had to make another difficult decision. He had

been talking with his brother, Patrick, about a business idea. Patrick was especially brilliant in woodworking. Both of them were highly creative, being visionaries and inventors. Lively conversations in sign language almost always revolved around a creative idea. Visions for designing and making kitchen cabinets were especially inviting. Daniel would layout the pattern and Patrick would build them.

He knew he would enjoy working with his brother. They would be helping each other, and the hours would hopefully be less draining on the family. Daniel sensed that it was time to leave the restaurant business and embrace his dream of working with his brother.

Daniel and Patrick not only designed, fabricated and installed cabinets for many kitchens; they were the first to bend Formica in order for the countertops to extend as part of the wall. They worked with some major manufacturers to make this happen. Successfully joining their talents and personal atributes they provided families with quality products for comfort and pleasure.

From Waterloo, Daniel and Mimi had moved to Canandaigua where they lived in the city before designing and building a home "out in the country." Although they worked very hard, recreation was also paramount. They hosted many parties for their children. With six children, Mimi made many heart shaped three-layer birthday cakes with fluffy homemade frosting and pudding in the middle. On one occasion, they gave Mary Jean a pizza and coke party. Bringing in a pizza oven, they made fresh, hot pizza throughout the party. It was always extra fun for the children at the parties when their parents joined in the dancing.

Daniel and Mimi enjoyed sitting on the porch, especially when the kids joined them. It was special for them to sit together outside after dinner for a sing-a-long. There were frequent softball games, bike riding, hopscotch games, sledding down the hills in the winter and badminton tournaments in the summer. It was always a great time when their nephew, Sammy, came to visit. Cousins Joanne and Sammy would play badminton, counting to see how long they could volley. They carried the game beyond the net, moving all over the yard, chasing the birdie before it could hit the ground. It was a big day when they volleyed to one hundred.

Donna and Sharon were so excited when Daniel called them out back to show them the see-saw he had made with planks and cement blocks. They were so proud and happy of their dad's great invention. He also made them a putting green in the yard using coffee cans. Making sure the children learned to take the game seriously, he carefully instructed them on the proper way to hold the golf club.

They also made frequent trips to Roseland Amusement Park and the ice skating rink and Aunt Bea's or Aunt Mary's cottage. Most weekends included time at extended-family gatherings. Through all the fun creations and long days at work, Daniel relentlessly faced the sickening images. Visions of the battles fought, long, cold walks, the starving, groaning prisoners, the bloody showers, the screams of the dying and exploding mortars continued.

With the bullet wound scar visible on his arm, Daniel was often faced with questions from his inquisitive children. When telling them about being shot, he focused on the miracle that happened after he prayed the rosary through the night. He told them about the sawdust bread and his attempts to get something to eat through the prison fence only to emphasize the importance of not wasting food.

The Purple Heart brought more questions. His answer was simply that he was awarded this medal for being wounded. The answers were as limited as possible, and sometimes Mimi offered the response. Yet, there was never mention of the battlefield and certainly no word of the Battle of the Hüertgen Forest.

In addition to the Purple Heart, Daniel received the Combat Infantry Badge for fighting in the Hüertgen Forest. He was also awarded numerous other accolades including the Bronze Star, European African Eastern, Conspicuous Service, Efficiency Fidelity Honor, Honorable Service while a prisoner of war, American Campaign, World War II, Expert Rifleman and

Ex-POW.

After Daniel and Roger were able to connect again, they committed to arranging visits every couple of years, taking turns traveling to each other's home. The family always looked forward to Roger coming to town. The buddies enjoyed their time together, sharing many laughs. They rarely spoke of the war, or their time in the prison camp; although they did tell the story about the escape attempt.

Using humor in delivering their rendition of this escapade brought some welcomed levity as they portrayed their physical condition while trying to run for their lives. In retrospect, they questioned their decision, sometimes referring to it as "foolishness." Yet, there was a confident understanding as to why it seemed like the right decision at the time. They conveyed an incredible brotherly bond of honor, compassion and trust — a priceless friendship.

Daniel was thankful to have someone who could relate to the prison camp experience with him. However, throughout the years he never met anyone else who fought in the Hüertgen Forest; despite the fact he had family and friends who had been in the war. In fact, many never heard of it. Daniel silently searched for someone, another survivor, who could relate to this battle.

Daniel became a life member of the Disabled American Veterans (DAV), where he spoke to many other veterans. Still, no one from the Hüertgen Forest Battle crossed his path. He was appointed Commander of the DAV and assisted in the organization of the first Veterans of Foreign War post in Canandaigua, New York. Daniel later served as the second Commander of that post. To this day, Daniel enjoys his meaningful involvement in the Ex-POW organization. Mimi frequently joins him for the supportive and fun gatherings. He is also a life member of Military Order of the Purple Heart.

Participating in the many parades was an important part of his post-war activities. He was always delighted to see his children having fun while he enjoyed the mutually supportive experience with the other veterans. Daniel was born on November 11, 1920. His birthday made the Veteran's Day parade extra special for the family. It was always a big deal to the kids that their father's birthday was on Veterans Day and their mother's birthday was on Christmas Day. No matter how many times it was said, the family always enjoyed the humor that the parade was also for Dad's birthday.

With the parades came the children's excitement and the anticipation of the fireworks. Unfortunately for Daniel, every boom of the fireworks reverberated to his core. He saw and felt explosion after explosion in the forest, reliving the images of the outcomes of these violent eruptions. Withstanding the brutal flashbacks, Daniel did not want to spoil the family fun. He never gave a hint of the scenery playing within him while most of those around him were exclaiming at a sight that they found spectacular. In fact, there was not any indication from any of the many veterans around him. How many inner battle scenes were ignited by the booming fireworks? How many veterans suffered silently, while others marvelled, oblivious to their plight?

Veterans from other areas would join in these parades. The Commander of the American Legion, who had been a classmate of Mimi's, lost an arm in the war. Every time Daniel saw him, he was continually reminded of how close he came to amputation. Frequently picturing how his life could have been, Daniel appreciated what he had in each moment.

Again with all the parades, ceremonies, gatherings and meetings, there was never a mention of the Battle of the Hüertgen Forest. At the same time he was working to provide for his family, serving other veterans and creating fun times with family and friends, Daniel continued to be alone in the embattled forest and prison camps; only recently has he heard of other survivors.

Inspired to work hard, Daniel was centered on enhancing the lives of others, creating pleasurable experiences and improving quality of products for comfortable living. Mimi was by his side, supporting every business venture. For many of Daniel's pursuits, he was ahead of his time. Pioneering ideas and products from an expanded point of view was highly challenging. Unfortunately, those around him often could not see as far as he could, nor had they seen what he had seen and survived. He knew the power of imagination and vision. He knew about maneuvering through muck, obstacles and chaos while overcoming fear, loneliness, impossibilities, powerlessness and hopelessness.

In the early 1960s, Daniel was involved in an innovative soft-serve ice cream business, featuring 52 flavors. Mimi, as well as daughters Mary Jean, Joanne and Linda worked with Daniel, sharing shifts at what was referred to as the "stand." The ice cream machine was set up to take an individual portion of a base flavor of vanilla or chocolate ice cream and add any additional flavor. A lever would whip the added flavor into the base flavor. Peanut butter ice cream was a hit, as was chocolate peanut butter and chocolate banana. Any kind of nut, fruit or flavor could be mixed with the base of vanilla or chocolate to create a new flavor of ice cream; with an ability to offer 52 flavors and beyond.

Daniel and Mimi worked long hours. Intent on refining the product, Daniel was always seeking the best chocolate ice cream with just the right consistency and flavor for the perfect ice cream cone. There were some who welcomed the expansive tastes of this sweet frozen treat; and the familiarity of vanilla and chocolate was more comfortable for others.

Disappointments and trials in the business world continued to bring valuable lessons. After attempts at different businesses, Daniel was drawn to solar energy. The oil crisis of the early 1970s shook people's sense of stability once again. Daniel and Mimi knew that in order to pursue this venture they would need to move closer to Rochester. Daniel believed that it was critical to explore alternative energy, and he knew the power that the sun held.

Daniel worked with solar energy systems, which he tested by heating the swimming pool water in the backyard of their new home in Fairport, a suburb of Rochester. He was sought out by some who were interested in being involved in this progressive venture with him. In fact, for some believers he installed solar panels to heat their swimming pools. At the same time, he was faced with those who questioned and doubted his ideas, often ridiculing him for thinking that such operative dynamics would work. Even if they understood the concept, they were of the opinion that it could not possibly work in cloudy Rochester. Once again, the world Daniel lived in was not quite ready for his vision of harnessing the sun's energy.

During this time, Linda, Daniel and Mimi's third daughter went to Germany. Prior to her trip, there was some conversation about the monastery where the prison camp was located. Daniel told her that it was in the Benedictine Monastery in Siegburg, though he did not think that she would be able to find the monastery. He was not sure if it was still there. However, being that she was his daughter, she persevered. Linda remembers her experience.

In August of 1974 I had an opportunity to go to Europe before I started graduate school. The first thing I thought of was to track down the monastery in Germany where they held my Dad captive during the war. With friends at my side, we found the monastery after a significant car ride from Berlin. It was off by itself, high on a hill. Slowly we moved closer along the narrow road to the then Benedictine Monastery. I wondered as I got out of the car how it must have been for him, walking up that steep incline exhausted, in pain, not knowing what would come next. It was very still and beautiful on a sunny summer's day. How could this have been a place of war and destruction? How could there have been so much hatred here?

We walked into the main entrance of this castle-like building to find a simple but large room. An L-shaped display case with a few shelves behind it was the only furniture. On display were several different types of liqueurs which the monks who lived there made and sold. We began to ask questions. We did not speak any German and they did not speak much English. I somehow communicated that my dad was there during the war as a prisoner. One of the monks recalled this piece of monastery history. He was very kind and understanding and brought me to an area that women were not allowed to enter. He proceeded with a tour of the private sanctuary. I felt blessed that I found someone so sensitive to break the rules and allow me the honor of seeing this space where my Dad had been so many years before. He was able to communicate (and I somehow was able to understand) that this was a special moment for him as well because of the respect and appreciation that he had for those that fought and survived and those that gave their lives.

On the way out, even though I had little money left, I did buy a bottle of liqueur to bring back for my Dad as well as a few pictures. He opened it and shared it with the family many years later on the eve of his only son's wedding and still has the bottle today.

Daniel was flabbergasted when she came home with the bottle of liqueur. There it was. A label displaying a photograph of the place where he had been held captive so long ago. This prison camp represented depravity as well as a stop on the road of survival. Since liberation, it had only taken up space in his inner world. Now, that Linda had walked where he had walked, this place of captivity seemed to move beyond Daniel's imagination. Bridging the different realms of reality, the family was now experiencing its existence with him.

While Daniel was working on solar energy, his daughter, Donna, received her lifeguard and water safety instructor certification. She told her parents of her idea to teach children swimming in their pool in order to help pay for her college education. She started with some neighborhood children. Soon the word spread that it was a small, personable place for children to learn to swim. Mimi saw how important it was for families and knew with how fast word was spreading, that Donna would need help. At the age of 52, Mimi decided to get her water safety instructor certification.

Mimi's dream had been to be a physical education teacher. She had only been at Ithaca College for a year when she was told that she had to come home to help her mother who was ill. Everyone else was working and her mother could not be alone during the day. Consequently, Mimi left her dream behind to take care of her mother. Despite the fact that she was never able to return to finish college, her passion for teaching children sports continued to burn within her. She was always ready to help kids have fun and achieve at sports. When her children were going to St. Mary's in Canandaigua, they did not have a physical education program. Volunteering her time on Saturdays, Mimi initiated and ran a girls basketball intramural program. She also shared her skills teaching younger family members how to swim and ice skate.

Now Mimi enthusiastically embraced this opportunity to work in an area that she both excelled at and loved. Mimi could work miracles with children who were terrified of water. Parents and students were thrilled with the results. The number of students quickly increased, even expanding to include some private lessons for adults who longed to overcome their fear of water. Mimi and Donna urged Sharon to get involved. With small classes of young and old, there were many smiles of fun and achievement at the Sunshine Swim Club. However, as the students were reminded to practice, many said that they did not have anywhere to practice.

The vision to create a family swim club was born. Daniel, Mimi and Donna, worked very hard to turn their dream into reality. Donna and Sharon were finishing college and needed to focus on completing their degrees and obtaining the experience for their chosen careers. There were frequent family consultations throughout the planning. In addition, Daniel and Mimi fought many battles with regulatory agencies regarding the acquisition of land permits. Persevering together, keeping their eye on the vision, they were able to make it happen.

In 1979, Daniel and Mimi opened the Turin Swim and Tennis Club in Fairport. They had created a space where they could both be involved in what they loved. Mimi expanded the swimming school and recreational activities. Daniel designed a solar energy system that heated the domestic hot water. After Dan, Jr. graduated, he joined his parents in operating the club. He helped install the filters for the pool and the computer system. He supervised the pro-shop and managed the snack bar. With Daniel's war disabilities, the physical demands of the club often called for his son's assistance in many critical areas. Dan, Jr.'s involvement and support was invaluable for them.

This delightful venture, filled with both trials and jubilation, offered many families and friends a place to enjoy fun together. Daniel and Mimi focused on nourishing mind, heart, body and spirit through the atmosphere and services they provided for family recreation. They had activities for parents and children both separately and together as a family. The parents especially enjoyed the adult social gatherings. Despite the hurried pace, Daniel and Mimi managed to meet the needs of the members. They always took time to appreciate the sight of families enjoying time together under sunny, blue skies, surrounded by bright flowers, and the laughter that floated through the air, filling hearts with many smiles.

They knew that in the distant, yet recent past, so many had suffered and lost their lives to make this possible. A life of love with family, friends, visions, business adventures, work, play and freedom were all so very precious to Daniel and Mimi. When they took another step on their life's journey into retirement, they had a deeper appreciation for all they had been given and grateful that they could continue to enjoy many blessings together.

Daniel and his family have continued to be in awe of the miracles that grace their lives. It was shortly after retirement, that Daniel fell and hit his head on the sidewalk while vacationing in Florida. He went to a local doctor who advised him to "take an aspirin and rest." When the headache persisted, they headed back to Rochester to consult with a neurologist they knew. Mimi drove most of the trip home, although Daniel attempted to help drive a couple of times but was feeling too ill.

Upon arriving in Rochester, Daniel immediately went to the doctor as his head was pounding incessantly. The doctor's evaluation revealed a subdural hematoma that did not appear to have a large amount of blood. Thinking it would resolve itself, he sent Daniel home. The next day Daniel's condition worsened, demanding that he return to the doctor. After examining him this time, the neurologist did not hesitate in ordering emergency surgery.

During this time and through the surgery, Daniel remained

remarkably steady and calm. Once again he was enduring extra-ordinary pain for days. Daniel's sense of humor brightened the faces of those caring for him during the procedure. After seeing the reality of Daniel's injury, the neurologist conveyed that without surgery he would have been dead the next day. Daniel relates that he knew his angels had never left him.

Throughout the years, Daniel continued to endure both the flashbacks, as well as frequent, severe, physical pain. The shrapnel remains in his back. As predicted by the Army doctor, the dislocated disk ruptured, which necessitated surgery in 1982. Still, he suffers from chronic back pain from the war injuries which occasionally make his leg numb.

The psychological residuals of Daniel's experiences were not addressed until decades later when he was given the opportunity to attend support groups. After many years of wondering why the frequent war imagery had not gone away, he was told that he had Post-Traumatic Stress Disorder.

With the VA meetings and gatherings with the Ex-POW organization, he has been able to share with those who could relate to what he was going through. He continues to find the Ex-POW organization extremely helpful and enjoyable. Although the war will always weave through his day to day life, no one has ever truly known the extent until now.

Daniel is not the only one who has been silent about the war, especially the Battle of the Hüertgen Forest. There are other survivors who began breaking their silence after over 55 years. Since these accounts began to be revealed, more information about the existence of this battle has been made available through books, films and websites.

Prior to this, other battles had received considerable attention through various media sources. Relative to other war conflicts, little was known of the Hüertgen Forest Battle. This is interesting in itself, considering the uniqueness of its conditions, intensity and tactical issues. There were 33,000 reported casualties from this five month battle in a 50 square mile forest (Chen, 2006). For perspective, there were 38,502 reported killed overall in the Vietnam War (United States, 2008). Due to the overwhelming number of deaths in the Hüertgen Forest and the controversial strategy, Daniel heard that many times soldiers were recorded as having died in the Battle of the Bulge, when in fact they lost their life in the Forest. After over 60 years, Daniel continues to be in awe that he lived through it.

Because so little has been written about the Hüertgen Forest and so few survived it, too few wives, parents, children, brothers, sisters and grandchildren of these soldiers know anything at all about the bravery and patriotism of their husbands, sons, fathers, brothers, uncles and grandfathers. They may know that they fought in the war or died, but they most likely do not know that they fought in a battle that is known to have exceeded the ferocity of most other battles.

To this day, Daniel is concerned about the many soldiers who were never fully recognized for the depth of their patriotism and sacrifice in the Battle of the Hüertgen Forest. Daniel often thinks of the young "kids" who gave their lives. He also wonders about those who were giving the orders, without regard for the reality, value or consequences of their orders. They were recognized for their service and have never been held accountable for their deadly mistakes.

The unspoken war strategy, which consisted of sending young men into battle without adequate training, weaponry, food, clothing or support to combat enemy tanks, mine fields and mortar shells, continues to tear at his heart. The strategists were the officers who gave orders without having experienced the horrific conditions of the Forest. These strategists were the generals, couched in comfortable quarters, who dismissed soldiers' pleas for dry socks, food and more weaponry to fight the battle. Their response was to tell the honorable soldiers to continue to attack without giving critical direction and information, without feedback from the field, knowing they were losing division after division, soldier after soldier, son after son, husband after husband, father after father, brother after brother.

The Forest had the appearance of a concentration camp with piles and piles of bodies. Daniel did not know or remember the names of the many young kids that he saw die a horrendous death on the explosive battlefield or suffer through the cold, agony of starvation, but he can never forget the faces of terror and painful longing that he saw in their eyes.

He is keenly aware that with such an incredible loss of life, there were too many who never heard the voices of their loved ones again. He thinks of the many who missed knowing their grandfather and so many soldiers who did not live to see their grandchildren. Daniel admits that he continues to grapple with the sadness and pain of surviving when others did not. Thoughts and emotions for these soldiers and their families have played a major part in sharing this story. Despite how uncomfortable it is to talk about this battle, his hope is to serve as their voice. He wishes he could truly convey the extent of their love and sacrifice. They bravely left all that was sane and secure to defend their country and loved ones, fighting the worst battle imaginable.

They died honorably for their country, and in this they were intensely driven by love for their families. The greatest love of all is that they gave of themselves to protect their families, to keep them safe. There is no greater love and no greater gift. Daniel's desire is that we all use the gift wisely.

Daniel has faith that the soldiers were not truly lost, for in their sacrifice they were guided to eternal love and liberation. He believes they found home in the arms of God. They live on through the gift of love which they passed on. As we live in love while cherishing the life of freedom, their spirits will forever be alive through what they gave. They did not die in vain.

It is essential that we diligently carry the spirit of love by living our lives with compassion, generosity and forgiveness. As difficult as it may seem, it is vital for survival. This is the true antidote to war for preserving our freedom; that peace may be victorious.

Daniel hopes that with the continuing evidence of the atrocities of war and the power of unconquerable, undying love, others will more fully live the truth of freedom — live dreams and visions, enjoy each other, love, laugh, move freely, create joy and simply be together. As we have seen far too often, none of these have been purchased without an immeasurable cost. Daniel has seen with great detail the price that was paid. Life has taught him that how we are with each other every day in the simplest of ways is related to our freedom and our peaceful survival. Daniel lives his life valuing the essence of the gift. He portrays faith and appreciation rather than worry and complaining, giving rather than taking, and patience and kindness rather than irritability and harshness.

Daniel prays that the military leaders who make decisions affecting the lives of others will have a heightened awareness of the consequences of their decisions and realize the importance of each and every human ordered into battle, including how critical it is to provide what is needed to fight the battle. Deep down he wishes that the military will recognize the true implications of decisions and learn from the Hüertgen Forest campaign and all battles. A soldier is more than a number of troops, more than a means to an end, more than one member of a division, more than a cog in a wheel and more than collateral damage. Soldiers are fellow humans with hearts and spirits, bound in love, intertwined with the hearts and spirits of family and friends.

Daniel sits back after humbly and courageously sharing his story. He speaks about the war after thinking over the years and the many times that he has relived the experience through flashbacks and memories. He shares his struggle in grasping the reality that he was the only known survivor from his squad. He is especially panged every time he thinks of the medic who died saving his life. He conveys his wonder that he actually walked from the battleground to the farmhouses. Even with his faith, he shakes his head in disbelief that he made that long terrorizing walk after fighting an indescribable battle. He again speaks of his surprise that the Germans did not just shoot him.

He reflects on the many miracles that he was blessed with and the many people he met who illuminated his experiences. He wonders about the German soldier who captured him, what was his life like? Would he remember Daniel? Did he think of the capture? Did he care about what he did? Daniel's face brightens with his sparkling eyes full of wonder. What would his life have been like without that German soldier? The soldier who kicked him back to consciousness, who did not shoot him on the spot, the soldier who showed him the way out of the Hell Forest without getting blown up. Would he have had a life?

Daniel again declared that without a doubt, God's angels were with him on the fiery battlefield, on the long walks and in the prison camps. He relates that he was sure angels were with him on the battlefield when the German soldier who captured him did not get rid of him immediately. Suddenly, Daniel's eyes radiate a deep realization, filled with an enlightened, meaningful awareness. "Do you think the soldier who captured me was an angel?" he pensively asks with a soft, gentle voice. He immediately responds to his own question, shifting in his chair with enthusiasm, "Yes! Yes! That's it! The German soldier was an angel, for if it wasn't for him…"

Daniel quickly recounts circumstances that exemplified his declaration. Despite the German soldier's cold, chilling eyes and inhumane treatment, without him he surely would have moved from unconsciousness to death being alone in the Forest with all of his squad killed. The German soldier also saved his life; he did not shoot him right then and there. He actually paved the way home. Daniel has moved to a place of healing, illustrated by his complete forgiveness. A radiating, profound peace filled the room.

The magnitude of this culmination is truly indescribable. Daniel takes a deep sigh, seeming to digest the intensity of it all. With great strength, he emphatically and gracefully rises from the chair, freely standing tall and straight, and joyfully exclaims, "Now, let's go eat lunch!"

For God has not given us a spirit of fear and timidity, but of power, love, and self-discipline. (II Timothy 1:7)

Daniel's Afterword

I have broken my silence. I have shared my story of what I and others lived through over 60 years ago in World War II. Although I had remained silent about most of them, these experiences are an indelible part of me. They continue to rise within me through flashbacks, especially with America's current engagement in war. There were times when I started to talk about my memories but stopped short, wanting instead to protect my family from the horror they represent. I had also hoped that if I did not talk about them, they would fade away; but they have not.

Likewise, it appears that other veterans from this battle were not able to speak about it for over 55 years. It was too horrific and uncomfortable to speak aloud. Now, through my involvement in this book, I have been reliving it in a different way. While moving back to the abhorrence of the forest and prison camp with great intensity, there has also been some relief. Compassion, caring and appreciation from family and friends embracing these experiences with me has brought healing.

Furthermore, I am concerned about other veterans who have also been waiting and hoping year after year, decade after decade for the sensational imagery to go away. To think about the immensity of war scenes, many much worse than mine, coming alive day after day within copious veterans, is truly staggering. I pray that in reading this, more veterans are inspired to open up and are able to find comforting relief. Additionally, I would like to encourage veterans of all wars to use the support services, especially the groups that are available.

Hopefully, through this book, others will benefit from a broader, deeper understanding of the daily conditions of war, and their profound impact on the soldier's life and their families' after the war. It is important to be aware of the unspeakable circumstances so many endured; the price so many servicemen, servicewomen and their families paid to maintain our country's freedom — a priceless commodity!

This account is a tribute to those who served on the front lines in the Battle of the Hüertgen Forest — all of those whose voices were silenced by suffering and death, all of those who did not get the recognition they so deserve. It is intended to honor all veterans who left this world on a lonely battlefield or prison camp and to their families who were left with a void.

I encourage readers to treasure their loved ones with an even deeper knowing of the sanctity and uniqueness of our lives. My wish is that there will be more movement towards appreciation of even the smallest comfort and opportunity. These are the life-giving decisions each of us must make, minute by minute, if we are to enjoy peace and happiness. In doing so, we are honoring God who gave us the gift of free choice when He gave us life. We are honoring all those who sacrificed so much to defend our freedoms, and we are respecting each other as human beings.

Though many stories have been written about the abomination of war, the actual living of these stories is beyond words. It defies description. For me to have survived when so many others did not, is incomprehensible and often painful to consider.

I have seen and heard of many situations where a GI missed death by seconds or inches, knowing they could easily have been on the very path where a fellow soldier met his fate. In their survival these American warriors are left to face the guilt of living.

Confused, soldiers speak of surviving as a matter of luck in an attempt to understand the inexplicable circumstances. Some are grateful for being blessed while others wonder where God was during times of incomparable human suffering and destruction. The elusiveness of survival and the faces of those who died are forever in the lives of veterans; we are never truly relieved of war.

While in the midst of a war caused by men hungry for power rather than peace, I was able to see God in action, not only for myself but also for others. At the same time, I am sorrowful for all who suffered horrendous imprisonment, torture, injury and death; to them, I am eternally grateful for their sacrifice.

This story contains a wealth of life lessons on faith and love that will not be found in a history book. I ask that it be passed on to the children so that my personal history of faith, love and miracles may inspire others to be a blessing to those around them.

Notwithstanding the brutal chaos, horror and devastation from which wars are fought, we are able to see God's miracles emerge. Knowing the suffering and sacrifice endured, brings a deeper understanding of God's wondrous works and appreciation of the valuable freedoms we enjoy.

I believe that I found the strength to share through love for my family. Mimi and I have been so blessed with six children and fourteen grandchildren, one of whom is now one of God's angels in heaven, and three great-grandchildren. I wish for them to know the breadth and depth of the love and faith that they are rooted in and the joy that they have given us.

My heart's desire is for people to respond to life's challenges with the wisdom of peace; for the fighting to stop. I pray for the never-ending power of true love and faith to be realized, bringing the joy of miracles to life and peace to all humankind.

"THE DAISY"

Barbed wire once enircled us and gave us
our physical limitations
but beyond the wire were daisys,
white, bright, and untrampled,
with centers of the sun, wild flowers of God.
Dear Lord, now that we have been gifted
with freedom from the wire,
give us strength and courage
to look to and beyond the daisys, Amen

Author Unknown

Sharon's Afterword

The reality of this forest battle, which was silently yet ferociously beating through our life, is revealed. I continue to digest the scope of the story that I had longed to hear for so long. The sound of Dad's words painting the maelstrom of war was both riveting and surreal. This was so very different than any war movie I had ever seen. It was more than any battle that I had ever heard of. It was so much more than I had ever imagined. Incredibly, Dad was literally in the midst of what has been called the "worst of the worst" (Whiting, 2000). Beyond rational comprehension, he made it home.

Shortly after beginning to work on the book, I realized that I was feeling more uncomfortable asking questions and encouraging discussions. When we began our conversations, I was convinced that it was best for Dad to share and get it out, and that it would be helpful and inspirational for others to hear. Now, with a heightened awareness, I did not want him to even speak through the ordeal again. I did not want him to have to feel the pain anymore.

Though he oftentimes declares that others "had it so much worse," minimizing his experiences, he was moved to open up in order to reveal God's miracles, love and the reality of those who fought the Hüertgen Battle. With every conversation, came an even deeper appreciation of his strong constitution in giving of himself to complete this book. He patiently received every phone call to clarify details and check for accuracy. He opened himself to each meeting to discuss and review chapter after chapter, despite the evident distress the storytelling was evoking. There were times he simply had to say, "I need to stop now," only to stalwartly return at another time to ensure completion "before I leave this planet" and "for the kids."

Mom also humbly gave of herself in the sharing, writing and reviewing. This was the first time that she heard much of the story, including the Hüertgen Forest. With this came the sharp, penetrating realization that she had stored her own painful memories; she had not revealed her "war life" either. It was incredibly moving to see her make the connection in the timing of his capture and her heart wrenching premonition on Thanksgiving, 1944; to hear her speak of worrying about Dad on a bitter cold battlefield; to hear about the long months without knowing where, what or if.

With unwavering love and loyalty, she had sensed Dad's hidden pain through the years, while also living with her war traumas. My mother is a remarkable woman with extraordinary stamina, integrity and wisdom. She always insisted that this book not put any focus on her, as it was to be about Dad. She frequently minimized her profound influences on his survival.

At times I would wake in the middle of the night with nausea and a deep ache, suddenly being overcome with trembling and weeping as impressions of Dad's experiences rose within. There were moments throughout the writing when I was seemingly paralyzed with exhaustion. Knowing that the vehemence of these sensations, erupting from the swirling images, was virtually happening while I was safe and warm in my home heightened my astonishment that this was Dad's stark reality on so many occasions since 1944.

Now, I have a profound knowledge of why there has been silence. After Dad elaborated on his experiences in the Hüertgen Forest, I researched this battle on the web. I read that it was considered "the worst of the worst," "the heaviest campaign ever witnessed," and a "wild and weird place." (Herr, 2006). It has been reported that "the Battle of Hüertgen Forest was the longest battle the Americans had ever fought in the history of the United States military." (Chen, 2006). These are just a few of many attempts to define the breadth and depth of this horror.

Reading reports of the forest battle and the intensity of the fighting struck hard as I digested the fact that Dad had described those very occurrences and conditions. I wept while pondering the unknown reality that had been embedded in my life; my father was truly there. He was actually one of those divisions after divisions. My father knew this secretive, most devastating battle firsthand. How could one depict through words this unimaginable massacre of young, promising, talented, honorable American soldiers?

The movie, *On Common Ground,* is one portrayal of the Hüertgen Forest experience. This documentary on the meeting of Americans and Germans who fought in the Hüertgen, reports that 33,000 Americans and 30,000 Germans were killed in this battle. The Germans shared very similar war experiences, speaking of the horrors of the battle as well as their fears and pain.

Yet, it was striking to hear the sadness as they admitted that their families think of them as killers and murderers not heroes as we think of our veterans. Reportedly, the sons and daughters of the Germans are angry and confused as to how their fathers could have taken part in the war. One German shared that his child wanted to know why he did not do anything to stop it. He responded by explaining what it was like to truly live under a dictatorship.

As horrific as going to war is, the value of freedom and patriotism, intrinsic to courage and loyalty, moves the American soldier to face ineffable danger and brutality. The Germans conveyed that the experience of fighting under a threatening dictatorship resulted in inconceivable post-war trauma. In addition to the painful memories, some were attacked with blame and shame by their loved ones.

It would be an incomprehensible tragedy if my father was met with anger and resentment from family and friends after all that he endured, or if we felt anything but compassion and gratitude towards him. I shudder to think of what it might be like for the Germans.

Now having some answers to the questions looming through my childhood, I am also keenly aware that there is much more that is too horrible to speak of. As much as I, and many others that I know, eagerly seek to understand these experiences, we must recognize what it is truly like for the veterans to share their war life. We need to be sensitive to the amplitude of the effects in giving voice to these long protected memories. Even as Dad reviewed the chapters, he expressed his amazement that he had actually gotten it out.

I pray this brings some understanding for many families of veterans who have had the same longing, the same questions, who never heard their soldier's story. Some asked the questions and were told, "I don't want to talk about it." Some simply knew not to ask. Some asked and received little, if any, response before their loved one passed away. I think of the residual effects on the thousands and thousands of families who lost their loved ones in the Hüertgen Battle.

Losing division after division compounds the casualties of the families. Family after family is left with a gaping hole, wondering, longing for insight or information to assuage this emptiness. Hopefully this reading sheds some light on this often disregarded battle, illuminating the momentous bravery of these shining soldiers. My desire is that it helps to free families from the cumbersome longing to understand their loved one's suffering; and that they are then able to embrace the eternal connection to each other's heart and spirit.

Within the misery of war is the dire need to know peace. Yet the sufferance of war appears to be permeating human existence, encasing the world. Peace is seemingly more and more elusive. This is demonstrated in the statistics that we hear on crime, divorce, disease, family violence, unemployment, economic turmoil and global wars. This is heard in daily conversations and events characterized by stress, irritability, impatience, harshness, financial woes, illness, conflict and hurt, fears and anxiety. All of this infers a severe lack of inner peace and a serious breakdown in living the fullness of freedom — impelling the need for a path to peace.

Throughout this story, my father's steadfast commitment to

love, faith and honor illuminates the way of peace. No matter what the despair, challenge or misfortune, Daniel demonstrated stamina, patience, compassion and integrity. These actions of love are the fabric of peace. The war and post-war challenges that my parents received did not sway them. They stayed true to who they are, their love for each other and family. I marvel at the degree of love, patience and appreciation that is naturally a way of life for them. I wish this could be easily taught or bottled and given away.

I know that their strong characters grew from the family foundation of faith in God. Who they are has evolved, not only from their accumulation of experiences but how they chose to respond to life's onerous circumstances.

What makes one person react differently to traumatic events than another? What makes one become bitter and full of rage while another is appreciative, thankful and forgiving? What makes one use the trauma to create opportunity while another turns to more limitation, degradation and destruction? What makes one become harsh, critical, impatient and destructive in times of stress while another demonstrates kindness, acceptance, patience and creativity?

I am so thankful for the choices that my father made rather than to allow himself to be consumed with the oppressive elements of anger, pain, despair and fear. The battles Dad fought, his near death experiences and valiant actions, moved him to a life of peace, and graced our family with many blessings. This rendition of a war experience is a testimony to God's presence, a soldier's faith and courage, the unconditional love of a man and woman, and a family legacy. Transcendent strength.

Throughout my life I have been driven to carry on the work of peace and healing. I see this passion to support people on their path to peace as a byproduct of what my parents taught me, as well as the undefined, unseen stirrings of war that I sensed throughout my life. The legacy that my grandparents passed on has been perpetuated by my parents' legacy characterized by love, faith, gratitude, integrity, forgiveness, selfless giving. Miracles. Peace.

One day after Dad and I had finished meeting about the book, I observed a silent wince of pain. I asked about it. He shared that his leg was bothering him. As I was leaving, I suggested that he listen to a healing CD that I had made focusing on God's love. While I explained the healing concepts in the meditation, he respectfully listened to me. In his humble wisdom, he smiled. I caught a glimpse of the twinkle in his eye and he caught my stare, we then shared a lighthearted chuckle. Dad nodded and stated, "I know." Of course, who did I think I was telling? It is everything that we have been speaking of.

As I drove away, I smiled with introspective joy and knowing. I have been honored and blessed with my father's commitment to the presence of God's love. The facts are that as this book is being written, my parents are in their late eighties, in good health and living actively and independently. Dad overcomes the war wounds and the residual stress of the trauma daily. His doctor says he has the heart of a thirty year old. I have a remarkably wise, patient, grateful, dancing, peaceful father who is a life-long Yankees enthusiast. Dad is able to see his captor as an angel of God. He is faithful, forgiving, funny and without bitterness. My sisters, my brother and I exist. This is the truth of the matter. My father is a healer. He is a peacemaker. He is a master of life. My father truly has a "purple heart."

Love is patient, love is kind. It does not envy, it does not boast, it is not proud. It is not rude, it is not self-seeking, it is not easily angered, it keeps no record of wrongs. Love does not delight in evil but rejoices with the truth. It always protects, always trusts, always hopes, always perseveres. (I Corinthians 13:4-7)

These are the lyrics of a song that Daniel and Mimi's children commissioned for them for their 60ᵗʰ Wedding Anniversary.

A Special Romance

A summer dance at Crystal Beach
That's where you met
A '41 blue torpedo
You can never forget

Now you share a lifelong love
It was your faith in God and each other
Today you celebrate 60 years
Of being together

You have a never-ending love
A special romance
You show love for each other
At every chance

By cutting a grapefruit
Or just playing sixes
You still start your day
With good morning kisses

You've devoted your lives
To each other's success
To each other's dreams
And happiness

You have always been there
For your family
With support and understanding
Teaching respect and integrity

Dad, you survived prison camp
Mom knew that you would be safe
Your love to be reunited
Helped you both keep the faith

We know we are blessed
To have parents like you
And we're inspired to see this love
Shared by you two.

©Heart Song 2002
Anonymous, Rochester, NY

Five Daughters and One Son: Reflections and Impressions

These personal expressions were written independently from the book and each other.

Mary Jean shares:

Of course, I was too young to remember my experience of being the first born of a father who was in the prison camp during World War II and of a mother who had to endure the agony of her husband going to war when her first child was going to be born. I believe my mother's worry and sadness affected me in the womb. I heard about how I cried when my father, a stranger to me then, first saw me.

My dad did not talk very often or in much detail about what happened in "that world" when I was growing up. But there was one overwhelming experience that I always felt during my childhood, while I was an adult, during my marriage and to this day. It permeated my entire being and was most influential in shaping my persona. It was the experience of my mother and father's love, for each other and for their children.

Joanne shares:

The bullet, the bread, the Purple Heart in a velvet covered case. The kind smile of a gentle, loving father. I recall the musings and wonders of a young girl trying to understand the pieces of information shared with me about how a healed over, glossy wound happened. For many years I was unable to articulate or understand the feelings of confusion and sadness— that my father whom I loved so dearly would have endured such pain. As I grew older and began to understand the concepts of war and the scale and suffering of "The War," the threads that wove our family which contrasted so dramatically became clearer to me. I do not know what prompted him to begin to share his journey with his grandchildren following a Thanksgiving dinner. I do know that it has given me profound insights and some clarity to the cloudy confusion I grappled with as a child. I began to understand his priorities and values that became clearly etched in his heart and soul during those long dark days in the prison camp. I could feel the experience of how he lived his life and parented his children with strength, dignity and a gentle love that spoke daily of his gratitude and appreciation. I now often reflect with sadness — thinking of the pain he carried, silently remembering the horror, unable to share and not appreciated by even the closest family or friends. They could never measure the hero this man was, the kindness and caring he showed the young soldiers as they died around him; those whose lives he saved through his faith and determination. What I do know now as an adult, daughter, wife and mother, as the pieces come together and an understanding is achieved that my father valued his family and his faith beyond any material measure, that his integrity and honesty would never be compromised by greed or ambition and that his love and devotion for his wife and our mother would never falter.

Love, Faith, Forgiveness. Transcendence.

Linda shares:

My memories and experiences of my dad, prisoner of war:
As a very young girl I remember sitting on my dad's lap fingering the scar on his forearm asking him if it hurt when the bullet hit. He promptly calmed my fears and assured me he quickly healed so he could come back to his family. There was a roll-top desk at the bottom of the stairway that had a hidden compartment. My sisters and I knew that inside the small drawer tucked away behind the little door was a blackened, hard, rather cubed looking object that he said was a piece of bread. My dad said it was made out of sawdust and that was what they gave him to eat. The Purple Heart was kept close to him but tucked away in the bedside stand drawer upstairs in his bedroom. I remember quietly and reverently opening the drawer and lifting the purple velvet box top to peek at the heart shaped medal inside.

I grew up watching my dad. Everything I saw influenced who I am today. Watching him in church and his diligent participation as a member of the Catholic Church led to my deep spiritual commitment. This has guided my life journey. Watching him and helping him build things around the house kept me open to creativity. Observing his multiple business ventures that were always ahead of their time taught me the value of the pursuit of innovative thought. Experiencing his steadfast routine of waking us up each morning, making lunches and taking us to school when we missed the bus before he went off to work role modeled unconditional love and great parenting skills. He allowed us the opportunity to watch him in business and social situations which taught me the importance of trust, relationships and networking. His commitment to family, his love and respect of his parents and wife showed that the true meaning of life is in giving and not in receiving of material things. Hearing stories of his survival of the war taught me that hope, courage and perseverance can get you through the worst of life's experiences. His constant positive thinking and encouragement led the way for my career advancement. I cannot think of part of my life that was not influenced by my father.

Donna shares:

My dad is brilliant, sensitive, honest, funny, artistic, visionary, values-driven, creative, thoughtful, hopeful, faithful, courageous, and a wonderful human being. I am constantly amazed at how his world is always growing, expanding, and engaging new thoughts and ideas. I know that these special innate qualities were the source of his survival tactics as a POW, and his unending faith in God, and in God's miracles, were the reasons for his survival. My dad's story needs to be told, so everyone can understand the strength derived from a fundamental faith in God's goodness, especially when one is surrounded by wickedness and evil. My dad never gave up hope, and throughout his horrific ordeal he never let go of his vision of returning home to live life with my mom. He was determined to survive, despite all odds. I will forever be grateful for the life lessons I learned from his resolute spirit and his demonstrable belief in miracles. I love you, Dad. Thank you for coming home.

Sharon shares:

Ever since I can remember, I longed to hear the war story. It was the mystery that tugged at my heart throughout my life. Bits and pieces of the story came through on various occasions, but not about the battlefield. My desire to know more was directed to the war movies that I was drawn to when I was younger. I remember trying to picture Dad actually being there, wondering what it was like for him, what he saw and how he survived it. I kept trying to comprehend his ordeal beyond the movie. When my brother played with his GI Joe action figures, I wondered what Dad was feeling watching him. It was not just play for him. I often wondered what it felt like to be shot. Finally, I asked him, and he simply replied, "it burns." It was always a special time for me whenever I held the Purple Heart or touched it. I was always so proud for any opportunity to tell someone about my dad who was shot, received a Purple Heart, and was in a prison camp in World War II.

Also, I recall the great sadness whenever images of Mom alone not knowing where her husband was, and typing alone in the dark came to me. I had a sense of her loneliness and fear. At the same time, I so admired her stamina and courage, in using the darkness as an opportunity to create.

My desire is that Dad and Mom know how much they are appreciated for all they have done and continue to do. This is a heartfelt recognition and expression of gratitude for suffering for us; for persevering and overcoming the agony of the trauma of war to give so selflessly and creatively for our family; for all the inspirational and valuable business experiences; for all the creative fun and frolic, for all the words of wisdom, for teaching me about overcoming fear with love, patience, appreciation, compassion and faith in miracles. Your true brilliance, depth of character, courage and love for each other has tremendously impacted me. Thank you for illuminating the richness and the profound meaning of our lives. I thank God for the blessing you are.

Dan, Jr. shares:

Dad,

In my eyes you are a true hero. Your passion for life and family have been an inspiration to me. I can still remember how proud I was showing my friends your medals and retelling the stories of you being a POW. I cannot even imagine how Mom felt during your time away. I'm sure that her living through those hard times helped make her such a strong, devoted, loving woman and mother. She is also such an inspiration to me and our family. To stand by you and with you through my life has been a beautiful experience. I can only hope to be as good a father as you are a great father. To be able to teach my children about life, integrity and honesty as you taught me. I thank you for your service to our country. You truly represent the finest of The Greatest American Generation. I love you and Mom so much. I am proud to have you and Mom as my parents. I am proud that my son and I carry your name.

Love, your son, Dan, Jr.

Works Cited

Chen, C. Peter. "Battle of the Hüertgen Forest."
World War II Database. April 2006. April 2006
<http://www.ww2db.com/battle_spec.php?battle_id=117>.

Herr, Ernie. "The Worst of the Worst: Battle for the
Hüertgen Forest." 5th Armored Division Online.
Jan. 2006 < http://www.5ad.org/hurtgen_joe.htm>.

On Common Ground: An American-German WWII Reunion
(2001). Dir. David Eilenberg and Jessica Glass. 2001. DVD.
Arrow Film & Video Inc., 2003.

United States. U.S. National Archives and Records
Administration. Nov. 2008 <http://www.archives.gov>.

Whiting, Charles. The Battle of the Hüertgen Forest.
Cambridge: Da Capo Press, 2000.

108